THE MEASURE

OF *Success*

CAROLYN McCULLEY with NORA SHANK

THE MEASURE OF *Success*

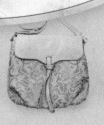

UNCOVERING
THE BIBLICAL
PERSPECTIVE ON
WOMEN, **WORK,**
& THE HOME

B&H
PUBLISHING GROUP

NASHVILLE, TENNESSEE

978-1-4336-7992-6

Published by B&H Publishing Group

Nashville, Tennessee

Dewey Decimal Classification: 248.843

Subject Heading: SUCCESS \ HOMEMAKERS \
WOMEN—EMPLOYMENT

1 2 3 4 5 6 7 8 • 18 17 16 15 14

Contents

The LORD is gracious and merciful,
slow to anger and abounding in steadfast love.
The LORD is good to all,
and his mercy is over all that he has made.

—PSALM 145:8–9 (ESV)

Preface

You probably picked up this book because you have questions about work, success, and family life as a woman. I have been thinking about the topic for decades myself. I grew up in the midst of the women's liberation movement of the 1960s and 1970s, studied journalism and feminist women's studies in college, and then became a Bible-believing Christian at age thirty—which shook up all my prior assumptions about being female. I've worked all my life because I had to support myself as a single woman. I have a high view of marriage and motherhood, even though I've never had children of my own. And I've traveled extensively to other nations, where most of my American ideas and assumptions have been challenged. In other words, I've been all around the circle when it comes to the issue of being female and what we "should" be doing as women.

In a way, this book is the third in a trilogy. In my first book, I explored the concept of being a godly, fruitful woman who was unmarried.[1] I wrote it when I realized I was carrying around a silly notion that "real" womanhood was somehow conferred on those who got married and had children. That concept collided with the truth of the Proverbs 31 woman—a passage in the Bible that describes an incredibly competent, financially savvy, generous, hospitable, loving woman who is fruitful and does good "all the days of her life" (Prov. 31:12). That insight revealed I had been deriving more identity from an adjective ("single") than a noun ("woman"), which was not the emphasis I saw in the Bible. In studying what Scripture said about being a woman made in the image of God, I was released from my false concept that being single was somehow less feminine.

That project led to further contemplation of the meaning of womanhood and the publication of my second book, which was really the book I wanted to read as a new believer.[2] I wanted someone to explain to me the history of feminism—the good, the bad, and the ugly—and compare it with what I was reading in the Bible. How did our culture end up with so many contrasting definitions and evaluations of femininity?

In doing the research for my second book, I was startled to discover I basically knew nothing about the history of the home. I had no idea that my understanding was derived solely from a twentieth-century American experience, where the home was seen as a place to store your stuff and showcase your taste. I had no idea how profoundly the nineteenth century had influenced the role, place, and activities of the home. For most of history, the home had been a place of productivity and the small business unit of the local economy. By the twentieth century, it became a center of consumption. The public sphere—the marketplace—became the valued sphere. The private sphere—the place of intangible investment—became the devalued sphere. Yet all the activities of the private sphere were the ones that awaited eternal reward: the cultivation of loving marriages, the rearing and discipling of the next generation, the care for elderly or disabled relatives, and the mission of outreach to neighbors and hospitality for the church.

So what about that public sphere? Having written about biblical womanhood, marriage, motherhood, and the private sphere, I was left with one more area to consider. Ironically, right after the publication of my second book, I plunged headfirst into the world of small-business entrepreneurs by establishing a documentary film company in the depths of the Great Recession. It was a brand-new lesson in trusting God for provision and wisdom to manage others. As I was busy trying to keep my company afloat, my pastor suggested that I consider writing another book, this time on the topic of women and work. Overwhelmed with daily tasks, I laughed at the idea when he brought it up. But it took root and began to grow.

At the same time, I was receiving e-mails and calls from a friend whose life trajectory was very different from mine, but who had some of the same questions about women and productivity. I had known Nora Shank for a few years while she was single, but now she was a thirty-year-old married mother of two with a part-time business, living on the opposite side of the country. Whatever Nora found in the news or the blogosphere about work, she forwarded to me. As my inbox grew and our conversations lengthened, I realized our divergent life experiences were a great reason to collaborate. So we began brainstorming about this book.

I think it's no surprise that far more verses in the Proverbs 31 portrait are about productivity and financial management than relationships. In the biblical narrative, work is a co-labor of love, tasks done in partnership with a gracious God who uses our labors to bless others. In response to criticism that He healed a sick man on the Sabbath, Jesus said, "My Father is working until now, and I am working" (John 5:17 ESV). His work was to glorify His Father and help others. Ours is the same. That is the definition of our productivity.

Should women work? Absolutely! Women should work and work hard every day. As Christ-following women, the Bible calls us to work for the glory of God. But the *location* of where we work is neither the definition nor the measure of our success.

Is this a book about women working in the marketplace? Yes. Is this a book about women working at home? Yes again. What follows is our exploration of how this looks for different women at various stages of life. We believe there is much wisdom to be mined from the Bible to help us think about love and labor throughout the entire arc of a woman's life. Therefore, we have segmented this book into three sections: the story of work, the theology of work, and the life cycle of work. The story of work is the biblical and cultural histories that have shaped the way we work today. The theology of work is an exploration of four fundamental concepts of work. The life cycle of work is where we take what we've learned in the previous sections to explore how to apply wisdom principles to various seasons and stages of a woman's life.

Finally, thanks in advance for your patience with the limited illustrations in this book—we couldn't possibly address every scenario or situation, but we hope there will be enough commonality in this book to inspire you in your particular situation. We also apologize in advance for the awkward terminology of "stay-at-home mothers"—we know how hard stay-at-home mothers work and yet we don't have a better phrase to offer. Because many of the stories we share are sensitive, we changed all of the names and a few of the identifying details in this book. But the facts of the stories are accurate and verified by those who graciously shared them with us.

No matter where you work right now, we trust you will find encouragement in the pages that follow to be a creative, fruitful, and industrious woman for the glory of God.

The Story of Work

CHAPTER 1

Our Story

When my mother passed away after a car accident, my sisters and I had three days to pull together my mother's funeral. Planning a funeral is like planning a wedding on steroids—you have to shape the ceremony and coordinate all the details of the reception, only in less time. And while grieving.

As we sat around in our pajamas frantically planning it all, I had the difficult task of writing my mother's obituary. I volunteered to do that because I wanted to honor her life. But writing her obituary presented all the challenges I had wrestled with as I worked on this book. The last words about my mother's life were to be about her occupation, when I knew that was only part of her identity. When her life was processed through the standard obituary template, it only handed back the labels of "homemaker and volunteer."

At least it wasn't "housewife." She was always outspoken about that: "I am not married to a *house*."

My mother parented me through an upheaval in women's identities during the years of the women's liberation movement. Though she worked for years in television and newspaper jobs, after she married my father, my mother chose to work at home, rearing three daughters and making a home for our family. During the 1960s and '70s, the choices she made about productivity were questioned by the larger culture, making her feel irrelevant at times.

I have never married nor had children, and have always worked. When people hear that I'm an author and filmmaker, I nearly always receive an enthusiastic response about how interesting my work must be. Sometimes I feel what I do is perceived as more interesting than my mother's work. But as much as I enjoy what I do professionally, I've always wanted to have a husband and children too. It's not an either/ or decision, but sometimes it feels that way—especially when people I've never met assume I've purposefully made the choice to be a "career woman."

My sisters were both professionals who continued working after they got married. But not too many years later, with three children each and seriously ill in-laws, they each chose to step away from the workforce for a number of years to take care of their families. Their days are full with an endless list of care-giving tasks for multiple generations.

We are one family with multiple examples of female productivity. But for my entire life, all I've heard is what women "should" be doing. There's always a new controversy erupting. As I was working on this book, one top technology executive was rounding the speaking circuit telling women how to be more ambitious. Another top technology executive built a nursery next to her office and returned to work after a mere two-week maternity leave. Then she ruffled the "sisterhood" by recalling the work-at-home privileges for her employees. A third woman, a successful professor, published an article seriously skewering the idea that women can have it all. Each time, factions from multiple perspectives fired warning shots into the blogosphere that these were untenable ideas.

Individual skirmishes in the "Mommy Wars" always have collateral damage—wounding weary women who are trying to do the best they can with the resources, opportunities, and responsibilities that they have.

We need perspective.

There's a good lesson to be learned from an idea that arose 100 years before the first volley in the "Mommy Wars." It's the concept of a flat earth.

Most of us have been taught that our ancestors believed the earth was flat because the early church believed that to be true. But in fact, the idea of a spherical world had been accepted as early as the fourth century BC.[1] Anyone who ever watched a boat sail over the edge of the horizon and return could never have believed the earth was flat.

So where did the false idea develop that the church believed that the world was flat? It was revisionist history made up during the late nineteenth century. Two books were published around 1870 with this "fact," in order to stigmatize Christian beliefs and support "scientific" thinking in the battle over evolution. After their publication, nearly every secondary-school textbook in America featured that "fact," even if diligent study of historical materials and common sense dictated otherwise.[2]

Truth was squashed to serve an ideological agenda.

As twenty-first-century women, we also have been handed a number of "flat-earth facts" about our lives that we accept without question—from people on all sides of the issue. It can be hard to discern them except for one factor: you can recognize a "flat-earth fact" by the one-size-fits-all box that it comes with.

The pain that comes from trying to squeeze into someone else's one-size-fits-all box can be excruciating. Just when you've almost got yourself all stuffed in, someone comes along to kick your box over.

> *You're a working mom?! You must really neglect your children!* THWAP!

> *Oh, wow. You're one of those homeschooling moms. Are all these kids yours?* THUD!

> *So you're not coming back to work after the baby is born? Huh. Well, good luck with that.* BAM!

> *You didn't take that promotion so you could be home for dinner with the family? How's that working out for you?* BOOM!

> *Yeah, single women who are successful in their jobs are . . . intimidating.* KER-POW.

> *Oh, so you are a stay-at-home mother? Yeah. Um, I guess that's cool.* SPLAT.

Relax. This book is not another one-size-fits-all box.

In fact, I am passionate about calling out "facts" that are based on one-size-fits-all thinking. Especially when the advice is applied broadly to all women at all times, no matter their training, circumstances, location, gifting, or personal histories.

The only way to be freed from this endless cycle of misunderstanding is to see how we got here—*and then cease measuring each other by human standards.*

I am passionate about calling out "facts" that don't line up with the grace, mercy, and freedom offered to us in the gospel of Jesus Christ—especially for those who have never heard that good news! That's why I wanted to write this book: to help women in all stages of life think clearly about the God-given gifts and opportunities they have, and how to invest those individual and specific situations in light of eternity.

This is a deeply felt issue for most women. I was reminded of this when I was asked by a large church to speak at a women's retreat on the topic of women and work. Other speakers addressed women in the home and women in the church. It seemed like an event with something for everyone. Yet after I spoke, I kept hearing how many women didn't show up to *the entire retreat* because they feared that my one session on women and work would chastise them for their choices. Those who spoke to me afterward said they wished their friends had heard what I said about the broader picture of female productivity: "What you had to say wasn't about being a working woman or a stay-at-home mom—it was for all women."

This wasn't the first time I had encountered this fearful confusion. Years ago, when I first began to speak about issues related to Christian women, I always honored the roles of wives and mothers. I was a single woman who was employed full-time, a fact that was a part of my speaker introduction. Nevertheless, I could always count on someone raising her hand and asking, "Is it okay for women to work outside of the home?"

We are shouting at each other over the walls created by a number of "flat-earth facts" because we don't know the history of women's work. We accept the one-size-fits-all boxes when we don't have to. What we really need to know is the purpose of work or how to think about the multiple facets of productivity that make women's work different from men's. This isn't a new idea. What we really need are timeless wisdom principles straight from Scripture.

How Then Should We Succeed?

If you've opened this book expecting someone to hand you a template for a successful life, you won't find it here. What you will find is an overview of women's work throughout many eras, an exploration of what it means to be made a woman in the image of God who is to be fruitful at home and work, and some ideas about how to apply these concepts in various stages of life. But no templates for professional or personal success. That's because the true measure of success is not based upon any human standard.

Our culture creates identity out of productivity and rewards what it perceives to be more important or of greater status. Jesus did not make this mistake. He modeled servanthood for us so that we could understand the hierarchy of His Kingdom. As He told His disciples: "You know that those who are regarded as rulers of the Gentiles dominate them, and their men of high positions exercise power over them. But it must not be like that among you. On the contrary, whoever wants to become great among you must be your servant, and whoever wants to be first among you must be a slave to all. For even the Son of Man did not come to be served, but to serve, and to give His life—a ransom for many" (Mark 10:42–45).

Our culture believes that we are self-made people and that we can achieve whatever we want to do. But the Bible emphasizes over and over again that we are merely recipients of grace. All that we have is a gift from God. First Corinthians 4:7 says, "For who makes you so superior? What do you have that you didn't receive? If, in fact, you did receive it, why do you boast as if you hadn't received it?"

How then should we measure success? We should think as recipients who will one day give an account for how we managed what we were given. We are stewards of all that we have received, including our relationships. It is God who gives us the spouses, friendships, children, time, talents, interests, opportunities, and tasks that fill our days and years.

We may be wives or mothers, but as important as these are, they are roles that end in this life. We continue on into eternity as children of God and sisters to those who have been rescued by Christ.

We may work in highly esteemed professions or we may not be paid for our daily labors. Those roles are not our identities, either. They are merely opportunities to be invested for the glory of God. Those things God gives us in terms of relationships and opportunities, He wants multiplied for the sake of His kingdom.

That's the true measure of success—and the message of the rest of this book. But right now, my collaborator, Nora, and I want to introduce ourselves to you through our stories of love and labor.

"A Huge Color TV"

When I (Carolyn) was a little girl, I would go with my mother to visit one of her friends. This woman lived in a convent and had the biggest color television I had ever seen. So for a while, whenever any-one would ask me what I wanted to be when I grew up, I'd promptly respond: "A nun. They have a *huge* color TV!"

My first vocational choice was obviously not a well-researched one.

Nor was my plan a few years later to become an Olympic gymnast. I was neither petite nor particularly coordinated. I had a surplus of enthu-siasm but a serious deficit of skills.

As an adult, the convent theme resurfaced. I was in my early for-ties, childless and single, and spending Christmas with my parents—while my married sisters were with their own families. As we sat at the breakfast table on Christmas morning, my mother looked over at me and said, "You know, your father and I are concerned about you. When we're gone, we want to know that you are taken care of. So, I'm wonder-ing . . . would you consider joining a convent?"

Not the best timing for a single woman's emotions, perhaps. Christmas has all kinds of expectations wrapped around it. But I give her props for being concerned about me.

"No, Mom, I hadn't considered that. I guess because I already have a huge color TV," I said.

Ha! Okay, that's what I *should* have said, but I actually didn't think of it until years later. That would have been a snappier answer. I only thought to myself, "A convent? *Really?*"

Though the convent was the only option for most unmarried women in the Middle Ages, fortunately I had a few more vocational options in the twenty-first century.

For more than thirty years, I've been employed in several positions in television and film production, print publishing, and corporate com-munications. Which is an amazing feat, since I continue to maintain that I'm only twenty-nine. (Don't laugh. It only encourages me to keep trotting out that line!)

Most recently I launched my own film company. The year that I started, the economy unraveled faster than I could write my business plan. I had already given notice at my previous employer and was only a few months away from concluding a position I had held for a decade. The news headlines made my head spin as we spiraled toward the bottom of the Great Recession. I clearly remember a sense of doom, wondering if I had made the right decision.

The industry was undergoing a major change in how films were marketed and distributed, and I didn't want to miss the opportunity to ride this wave. That was the exciting part. The bittersweet part was that I didn't expect to be an entrepreneur in my mid-forties. I had expected to be like my younger sisters: married with three children and spending most of my time in a minivan. We were all incredibly busy at this stage of life, but my busyness didn't yell "Mom" at me.

Ten years earlier, I had made a similar leap when the production company I worked for in Virginia had closed down. I was a new Christian and knew that if I were to remain working in the film industry, I'd have to move to New York or Los Angeles. But I decided to stay put for the sake of my church. I hoped that one day I'd have the privilege of being a wife and mother. Prior to my conversion at thirty, I didn't have a very high view of marriage. But after becoming a believer, I had a new appreciation for it. So with bright, shiny hopes, I transitioned my film career to a freelance writing career. In my mind, it was the perfect profession to integrate with family life: easy to do from home and something that could be ramped up or down as needed.

Pleased with myself for devising a flexible career, I waited for the husband and children to show up. When they didn't materialize after a few years, I eventually went back to work full-time. I needed the money. I still hoped for marriage and family, thinking I could always fall back on the freelance writing experience if needed.

Unfortunately, my long-range plans didn't include the idea I would remain single. Ten years later, I was in my mid-forties and needing to activate a fallback plan I didn't have. That's when I decided I would take the plunge as an independent filmmaker.

But hanging out your shingle as a freelance writer is vastly easier than creating a limited liability company with private equity and its myriad of financial and legal ramifications. My first year in business was a steep learning curve of SEC regulations, cash flow forecasts, and bookkeeping software. It was a faith-building exercise like none I had ever experienced. I learned what it means to pray for my "daily bread."

When you don't know where your next paycheck will come from, God's faithfulness becomes starkly vivid.

I'm now an employer with a small staff. It's not the same as being a mother, but I do feel a parental-like obligation to provide for my employees. Though my life didn't unfold to my own set expectations, I've seen God at work in my life in many ways. I have testimony after testimony of praying for a job, a contract, an invoice to be paid—and seeing it happen in nearly miraculous ways.

My work experiences have taught me that God is trustworthy. He has led me to take several risks as I've restarted my career at periodic intervals, but He has always been faithful to provide for me. These ventures were not free from worry, stress, or low finances, but they were instructive—especially about my own character. Work has been my crucible of sanctification. There's nothing that reveals a proud, impatient attitude quicker than a big project with a crazy tight deadline and a crazy small budget. "Love is patient, love is kind" (1 Cor. 13:4) is often most meaningful to me in the office.

As I have learned, God has a purpose for our productivity. He uses our daily labors as a means of grace to other people and a way to learn more about Him. I am fully aware I am living by grace and nowhere do I see that more clearly than in my work.

Making God Laugh

At the same time that Carolyn was starting her film company, I (Nora) called to ask her to write a book for women about work. The growing tide of questions in the media and public eye, as well as my own inner struggles, had prompted my interest. We had a very long phone call.

What we came to find out was that though we had divergent life experiences, we agreed about the problems we faced with work as Christian women. We found that many of our ideas, expectations, thoughts, and feelings about work intersected, despite the fact that I did marry and have children.

I love and value the roles of wife and mother, but work has always been an important part of my life. Starting out, I thought that my career as a dietitian would be a nice launching pad into and between those roles; but now, I know how little I knew about work as a young woman.

Growing up, I belonged to the generation raised in the sweeping effects of feminism's victories. It also helped that it was an age of unprecedented prosperity. To find a job that you were not only educated to do, but that you felt fulfilled in, was the embodiment of our dreams.

Girls my age believed we could do it all, and be everything we could aim for: "Be the first woman president!" and "Go change the world!" we heard. We had the rights and we just had to climb our way up the ladder of success.

But dreams like those don't last very long. Ladders break. People forget to hold you underneath. Plans change. I think that anytime you want to make God laugh, tell Him that you have a plan.

My plan was to finish college, get married, work for a couple years and then take time out to raise a family. I thought that the flexible work hours of dietetics in the medical profession would tie in well with my interests and my goals.

I remember the first time that I stepped into a room of dietitians. It was filled with women who were put together and confident. *Perfect,* I thought. *This is where I belong. These women are just like me!*

Going to that meeting that day made me think that I fit, that I found my spot with the right kind of job and the right kind of people. I had found something I could do, and felt like I was made to do it. Life was going according to my plan—I finished college, I got a coveted internship position, and now I was in a career stream I thought had the right direction.

When I was in high school, I swore that I would I finish college. In my private school, I was told that girls didn't need to have higher-level math requirements, because we were just going to be wives and mothers. That remark fueled my ambition. I didn't believe that, and neither did my dad. As the son of immigrants, he believed that education was a privilege. It was his dream that all four of us children would attend and graduate college.

While my dad encouraged me to pursue education, my mother was on the home front encouraging me to include marriage and family in my ambitions. Being a wife and mother were on my radar, but I told myself that I wanted more of what the world had to offer before I settled down.

It all came to a head the summer I finished my internship on the East Coast. As my program ended, I had broken up with my long-distance boyfriend, who lived in Texas. I had to return home to live with my parents—without a boyfriend, a job, or a direction. I felt let down by the dream.

My faith hit the wall of reality. I thought that because I had worked so hard all those years in high school and through college that God owed it to me. I thought, *If you work hard, it works out for you.* I thought this was not just my plan, but *the* plan God has for good Christian girls.

This is where I think God began to laugh. Especially when I started dating one of my "I nevers." After my previous experience, I had said I would never date another guy long-distance. "It's too hard," I told myself. Yet this man, Travis, who would later become my husband, won me over with his encouraging words, despite the 3,000 miles between us.

It turns out that God had a different plan than my own, but it was better than I expected. Jeremiah 29:11 (NIV) says, "'For I know the plans I have for you,' declares the LORD, 'plans to prosper you and not to harm you, plans to give you hope and a future.'" The verse that was repeated to me throughout my childhood, now made more sense as I saw God directing my initial life choices. No matter what I said I would do or not do, God always found a way to convince me that what He had was infinitely better.

I would need that when I grew up.

Lessons in the Desert

After Travis and I were married, I moved out to Arizona, where he was living at the time. It wasn't easy to start over. We not only had to build a new marriage, but I had to rebuild everything I once had on the East Coast. Even so, I figured I was back on track with my life goals.

During my seven years there, I worked as a registered dietitian with two sister hospitals. I saw patients in the hospital, spent time building a community outreach nutrition education program, and put in extra effort to develop a private practice. I enjoyed my work.

But this was still the Wild West, made worse by the Great Recession. Despite the success of my job, we were affected by numerous circumstances we couldn't control. We moved five times. My husband had seven different jobs. We had two surprise babies. We were on unemployment twice. From the outside, we probably looked like we were living the American dream: we were married, we had two kids, and we had bought a home. But when our van repeatedly broke down, living in the shop at least one week out of every month, instead of in our garage, it sucked our bank account dry. Then there were the humbling moments when we accepted money from family and friends to pay our bills. There is nothing about applying for public assistance that feels successful.

This was far from the idea I had about my life.

For a girl who grew up in a generation and place where every business venture caught like fire and ran at a profit, it was crushing. On the East Coast, I had run a profitable catering business for six years. Now I had to work just to pay the bills. *"Why can't one thing be easy?"* This is what I thought to myself on the mornings when I would pack up the car and the kids, drive them to their grandmother's, so I could rush to work and rush back home to them.

Once again I was confronted by my own expectations about work. I thought that work was about slowly achieving success, building something that got bigger and better. Here we were, two college graduates, my husband with a master's degree, and we were giving Christmas presents from a retail store where he picked up holiday work.

The lessons that I learned in the hard times really forged my dedication to the topic of this book. All my ideals about work or being a stay-at-home mom got thrown out the window during those years, like when I had to leave my eight-week-old baby at home with Daddy while I went to work. It made me want to learn more about work as a Christian woman. After my experience, I was even more convinced that young girls should get educated and have a skill to fall back on in hard times.

I had to go through the desert, literally and spiritually, to learn these lessons. I had to grow up out of these preconceived ideas about my life. I couldn't work because I had a point to prove or to fulfill myself. Travis and I together had to learn that we weren't owed anything, just because we worked hard or because we had advanced degrees. When life wasn't easy, we learned that we needed to work, not just for our basic provision or our own satisfaction, but that we had to do it for God.

A Fresh Start

We eventually found some footing. The economy stabilized and so did our lives. Oddly enough, my questions about work didn't stop when things got easier. In fact, my passion grew for this topic.

Travis encouraged me to be ambitious too. He left all his business books laying around and after leaving enough of a pile on the nightstand, I began to pick them up and read them voraciously. I thought, *Why aren't there any good books like this out there for women?* As my conversations with Carolyn continued, I realized that I really wanted to read a book like this.

But now I have new questions to add to the list. As soon as I thought I had everything figured out in Arizona—working part-time, managing my home, and with Travis having a stable job—we moved for a new opportunity and a fresh start. Now back on the East Coast, I transitioned to being a full-time stay-at-home mom for the first time in all the years we'd been married.

Staying at home with young children has dealt me a new set of challenges.

After working for seventeen years, I am wrestling with new angles on the same issues of productivity—but from home. Now I am asking: Should I work outside my home now that I don't have to? Is it wrong when I feel discouraged by how hard it is to be at home? Should I spend the next year investing into my profession before I have another baby? Should I even have another baby??

Now that my life has slowed down a little bit, I find I have to wade through a new barrage of pressures. Travis and I currently live in a very competitive area, and it comes with a lot of pressure to be a certain kind of mother. I am bombarded not only with all the cultural expectations for professional success, but I also encounter personal ones—like the ones for a perfect home and perfect children. The digital age only makes this worse. When the web plasters perfection everywhere, it's easy to feel intimidated by the comparison. It makes me ask, *am I doing enough?*

That's why the research we did for this book is helping me navigate my life today and the choices that I have to make in faith toward God, whether I work outside of the home or stay at home. What Carolyn and I both feel is that we need a bigger perspective of productivity. While our work lives are different, we see value in the work we both do. But we need to understand how we arrived at the idea that one was better than the other. Therefore, for the rest of the chapters in this section—the story of work—we will explore the history of women's work. Doing so will help us understand the assumptions we bring to our own narratives and the expectations we hold about work.

Carolyn and I are just two stories in the bigger narrative God is working to create. We offer them to you as a way to get to know us, and where we are coming from as we explore this topic. We recognize that our experiences give us blind spots. We know we are limited. We also know that our stories are unfinished. As God has been faithful thus far in our work, we know that He will be so for you too. As Psalm 33:4 (ESV) says: "For the word of the LORD is upright, and all his work is done in faithfulness."

CHAPTER 2

The Modern Story

I don't recall playing house when I was little. I definitely was an active little girl with lots of imagination, but I can only recall playing office or school. In those scenarios, I was always large and in charge! I was the teacher or the boss—never the student or the worker bee.

I pondered this memory aloud one night with my sister, an accountant and a mother of three, as we went over the financial statements for my film company. "Do you think it is significant that I never played house? That I never even *pretended* to be a mommy?" I asked, only half-joking. "Why wasn't this role on my radar screen as a young girl?"

I was a girl who grew up in the 1960s and '70s. As the adage goes, we're all a product of our times. If you are under thirty, my times are a large reason for whatever you are experiencing now. Interestingly, many women under thirty today really don't know what happened during the lives of those of us who have celebrated our twenty-ninth birthdays multiple times. The modern conflict between work and family definitely escalated in my life, but there's an even longer history of female productivity that needs to be dusted off and brought back for consideration if we are ever to understand how to think about life in our times. You can't understand where you are going unless you understand where you came from.

In this chapter, we'll look at recent history and how it shaped our current understanding of identity, ambition, the "empty nest" years and more. But then in the next two chapters, we'll rewind many centuries back to get a better understanding of women's work over time. The point of these chapters is to ground our current understanding of female productivity in a clear-eyed analysis of history. In later chapters, we will contrast that historical perspective with biblical teaching.

So hang with me here for a few pages of twentieth-century American history.

Mad Men, Mad Women

The year I was born, 1963, was a watershed year in many ways. Americans were restricted from traveling to or investing in Castro's Cuba. George Wallace became governor of Alabama and in his inaugural speech, he defiantly proclaimed, "Segregation now, segregation tomorrow, and segregation forever!" Betty Friedan published *The Feminine Mystique,* kicking off the Women's Liberation movement in the United States. The Beatles released their first album, *Please Please Me.* Martin Luther King Jr., delivered his "I Have a Dream" speech in Washington, D.C. President John F. Kennedy was assassinated in Dallas, Texas.

And Gloria Steinem was hired as a Playboy Bunny.

Contrasted to the defining cultural and political events listed above, Steinem's Bunny stint may not seem very significant. But Steinem did it to write an exposé about a job that was positioned as glamorous and empowering, but actually was demeaning to women—and not just because of the costumes they wore in the Playboy Clubs. Steinem's article revealed the labor conditions and wage abuses the Bunnies endured. The article elevated Steinem's profile and by the early 1970s, she was one of the leaders of the Women's Liberation movement and went on to cofound the feminist magazine, *Ms.*

Playboy reflected tensions in the contemporary workplace that affected both men and women. Ironically, Hugh Hefner founded *Playboy* magazine a decade earlier to rebel against the pressures men felt to conform to the breadwinner role. As one historian noted, Hefner tapped into the alienation some men felt in their jobs long before the women's liberation movement took off.

> In 1953, Hugh Hefner founded *Playboy* magazine as a voice of revolt against male family responsibilities. Hefner urged men to "enjoy the pleasure the female has to offer without becoming emotionally involved"—or, worse yet, financially responsible. In Playboy's first issue, an article titled "Miss

Gold-Digger of 1953" assailed women who expected
men to support them. Another article the same year
lamented the number of "sorry, regimented husbands
trudging down every woman-dominated street in this
woman-dominated land." By 1956 the magazine was
selling more than one million copies a month.[1]

Most people identify the turbulence of the 1960s as the turning
point in American history with regard to gender roles and family. In
many ways it was, but there was a long history that preceded it.

Manufacturing a New Normal

Some point back to the 1950s as the ideal and pine aloud for a
return to that decade. But if you pull back the curtain of nostalgia, you'll
find that the 1950s were a pivotal decade with a strong undercurrent of
upheaval. The Korean War, the Cold War, racial integration and the
civil rights campaign, communism paranoia, and the introduction of
rock music were the sources of some of these tensions.

What largely characterized the 1950s was how hard people worked
to create a "new normal" after the losses and upheaval of two World
Wars and the Great Depression. That "new normal" included new
ways of living as the economy strengthened. Starting in the late 1940s,
suburban sprawl dramatically changed the American landscape as millions of new homes were built. The economy grew quickly and by the
mid-1950s, more than half of the population had middle-class income
levels; by the end of the decade, nearly two-thirds of all American
families owned their own homes, 87 percent had televisions, and 75
percent owned cars.[2] This "new normal" is what we take for granted
now, but that rapid expansion of the middle class dramatically affected
mid-century American families. As one historian notes, family life was
always portrayed in a home filled with new consumer goods:

In the 1950s, consumer aspirations were an integral
part of constructing the postwar family. In its April
1954 issues, *McCall's* magazine heralded the era
of "togetherness" in which men and women were
constructing a "new and warmer way of life . . . as a

family sharing a common experience." In women's magazines, that togetherness was always pictured in a setting filled with modern appliances and other new consumer products.[3]

In the five years after World War II, spending on food in the United States rose by a modest 33 percent and clothing expenditures by only 20 percent, but purchases of household furnishings and appliances jumped by 240 percent.[4]

While advertising and television created the domesticated image of a family satisfied with its shiny new appliances, the current tensions of the "Mommy Wars" and the quest for work/life balance began to simmer. These items were advertised as time-saving devices, but the reality was that they only made the labor easier while also increasing the standard of cleanliness. Studies show the end result was that women spent more time with household work, not less.[5]

Ironically, women had once worked in the industries that were now selling them this "new normal." During World War II, the U.S. government ran huge propaganda campaigns to lure women into the workforce to help with the war effort. This campaign was run by the War Manpower Commission, a federal agency created to increase the manufacture of war materials. The government pushed magazines, motion pictures, newspapers, radio, and in-store displays to campaign for women joining the workforce. More than 125 million ads were run as posters or full-page magazine advertisements during this time. As the Basic Program Plan for Womanpower in the Office of War Information stated: "These jobs will have to be glorified as a patriotic war service if American women are to be persuaded to take them and stick to them. Their importance to a nation engaged in total war must be convincingly presented."[6] In response, more than six million women joined the workforce during World War II, taking on industrial jobs in places such as shipyards, lumber mills, steel mills, and industrial laboratories. (For African-American women, the majority of whom were employed in the service sector prior to World War II, the war effort only had a temporary effect. Their primary employment was and would continue for the next thirty years to be related to domestic service, with a smaller segment holding clerical jobs.)[7] As one historian noted, the range of jobs opened to women during the war was impressive:

> Millions of suddenly essential female workers took over male positions such as cabdriver, elevator operator, bus driver, and security guard. In one year, the number of female defense-factory workers increased by 460 percent, a figure that translated into 2.5 million women assigned to the unlikeliest tasks. Instead of making carbon copies or assigning homework, many women now manufactured tank parts, plane frames, engine propellers, parachutes, ships, gas masks, life rafts, ammunition, and artillery.[8]

And they were good at it. In May 1942, *Business Week* reported, "airplane plants considered women 50 to 100 percent more efficient in wiring instrument panels than men, due to general carefulness and a greater attention to detail."[9]

Once the war was over and the Rosie-the-Riveter campaign to attract women workers ended, the expectation was that women would leave the workforce. That didn't happen for many women. Only two years after the war concluded, the number of women entering the American labor force actually began to exceed the number of women exiting it. By 1952, there were actually two million more working wives in the labor force than at the height of the war, and there was a 400 percent increase in working mothers throughout the '50s. Part of this was a response to labor demand. Though employers had the right to require female employees to stay single as a condition of employment, the postwar economy needed women to fill low-paid clerical, sales, and service jobs. With so many women marrying young, there weren't enough single women to fill the demand. Therefore both employers and the government began relaxing their barriers to hiring married women. But most of the women entering the workforce then were over forty-five with the bulk of their child-rearing duties done.[10]

"Is This All?"

Then came the pivotal year of 1963, a year of two big firsts for women: Physicist Maria Goeppert-Mayer won a Nobel Prize for a mathematical model for the structure of nuclear shells—the first American woman to do so—and the Soviet cosmonaut, Valentina Tereshkova, became the first woman in space.

But despite these firsts, most women faced on-the-job limitations. In 1963, President Kennedy signed into law the Equal Pay Act, which prohibited "discrimination on account of sex in the payment of wages by employers." Then the President introduced the Civil Rights Act, which outlawed workplace discrimination because of an individual's race, color, religion, sex, or national origin. (It was passed in 1964, but wasn't consistently enforced for another decade.)

At the same time, Betty Friedan began her publicity tour for *The Feminine Mystique,* challenging the idea that women should be fulfilled solely as wives and mothers. Friedan introduced the idea of the "trapped housewife syndrome," reporting that housewives were asking themselves, "Is this all?" She was determined to change the role of American housewives, and she did accomplish this goal—igniting feminism's second wave in the U.S. (The first wave centered around the nineteenth-century campaign to obtain the right for women to vote.)

Friedan's book is considered to be among the most influential nonfiction books of the twentieth century. But historian Glenna Matthews says that though the book was important and profoundly affected its time, Friedan's arguments were flawed:

> *The Feminine Mystique* must be dealt with in two ways: as a document and as an analysis. In the first instance, the book is an invaluable source; in the second instance, its value is undercut by the author's lack of historical perspective. Friedan was angry about the developments of the 1950s and exaggerated the novelty of the suburban housewife's plight relative to earlier decades. Also, writing before the rebirth of women's history, she lacked any insight into the nineteenth-century version of domesticity.[11]

Too angry to be altogether fair, she assumed
that the housewife role was merely something from
which women needed to be liberated. She gave no
consideration to the issue of how many interesting
careers the society might have at its disposal, and
whether there would be enough to go around. Would
the woman who could only find a menial job outside
the home be that much better off than the housewife?
This, too, was an issue that Friedan ignored. Finally,
were there any components of the housewife role that
might be worth preserving? If there were, Friedan did
not mention them. Rather, she argued that women
needed "some higher purpose than housework and
thing-buying."[12]

For *sure*, women need a higher purpose than "housework and thing-buying"! But all forms of labor have their menial tasks. If you focus on those tasks alone, it's easy to lose sight of the grand goal of your efforts. However, Matthews is right in criticizing Friedan for not considering the current state of the workplace for women in the 1960s.

At that time, the "help wanted" advertisements were segregated by sex—"Help Wanted: Male" and "Help Wanted: Female." There were no laws against sexual harassment. Employers were legally entitled to fire a woman if she got married or pregnant. (In the case of flight attendants—a "stewardess" at that time—she could also be fired for gaining weight or existing beyond thirty.) Most women were barred from overtime pay or in some states from lifting more than thirty pounds, which limited the available jobs. Life was even tougher for nonwhite women, who faced both sexism and racism on the job and still had to work, anyway. Nonworking wives were also in a precarious position. At the time, only eight states gave a wife any legal claim to her husband's salary or property.

In December 1962, the *Saturday Evening Post* published a story about the state of American women, and included the survey of more than 1,800 American women conducted by pollster George Gallup. Gallup found "only two small imperfections" in the lives of 1960s American housewives:

One was what he described as the "rather plaintive" desire of wives for more praise from their husbands and children. One woman explained: "A man gets his satisfactions from his paycheck and from being asked advice by others. A woman's prestige comes from her husband's opinions of her. . . ."

Gallup's second concern was about what these women, now so focused on marriage and mother-hood, would do in "the empty years" after the children were grown. None of the respondents he interviewed mentioned this as a problem, but Gallup was troubled by their lack of forethought. "With early weddings and extended longevity, marriage is now a part-time career for women, and unless they prepare themselves for the freer years, this period will be a loss. American society will hardly accept millions of ladies of leisure—or female drones—in their 40s."[13]

Gallup's prescience about "the empty years" foreshadowed the feminist disputes of the 1980s and the "can women have it all" discussions of later decades. But in the early 1960s, what most affected women in the workplace was the "contraceptive revolution." As historian Stephanie Coontz writes, "The contraceptive revolution of the 1960s was a much more dramatic break with tradition than the so-called sexual revolution, which had actually been in the making for eighty years."[14] Five years after the FDA approved the first birth control pill in 1960, more than six million American women were taking the Pill. Two years later, more than 12.5 million women worldwide were taking it.[15] This fundamentally altered the time line of women's lives and challenged employment traditions that assumed pregnancy was always around the corner for women in their childbearing years.

Sequencing

Ten years after the women's liberation movement began, the upward economic trend ended. The year 1973 marked an international recession. Between 1973 and the late 1980s, the average real wages fell for the majority of workers, but men felt it most. Between 1973 and 1986, the median income of male-headed families fell by 27 percent, while women in service jobs saw their real wages rise. Thus in a difficult economy dogged by both recession and inflation, women's wages became necessary, even critical, for many families.[16]

Around this time, I began to read the daily newspaper. As a grade-school child, many of my assumptions about the world were shaped by the headlines of the day. From my young vantage point, it seemed feminism had won the war of the sexes—it certainly got a lot of press coverage. All that I read and watched seemed to be about women and work. So I grew up assuming I'd have a fabulous future doing something glamorous and interesting. I assumed work was my future, not motherhood, even though my own mother was home on a daily basis to watch me play office. Growing up with economic insecurity shaped my thinking, as well. I clearly remember our high school band taking advantage of the oil crisis following the Iranian Revolution to sell doughnuts to motorists waiting in long lines to buy rationed gas. Everything seemed so expensive and scarce, which was another incentive to make sure I could earn a living.

By the time I graduated high school and entered college in the early '80s, most of the legal barriers to equal employment and equal pay for women were gone. The wage gap between men and women still existed, but that was seen as an individual battle. During the feminist women's studies classes I took in college, we were taught to communicate assertively and directly and to negotiate our salaries—traits that were seen as masculine and one of the reasons more men than women succeeded in the marketplace. We talked a lot about the "old boys network" and sexual harassment on the job.

Even so, divisions in feminist theory were bubbling to the surface. In the 1980s, the feminism of the 1960s was viewed as being "assimilationist." It was focused on the fundamental similarity of men and women to promote equality and give women opportunities typically reserved for men. But in the 1980s, some feminists began to consider how women *as a group* were actually different from men as a group, and discussions arose about how to affirm that difference as legitimate and good. I recall debates about how feminists should actually push for establishing women's life cycles as different from men's—and normalizing that difference as good and acceptable. That was called "feminism of difference," but the term I recall hearing at the time was "sequencing." Instead of saying women should pursue the same time line and life cycle of men, "sequencers" argued for establishing a different time line for women—claiming that the truly radical notion would be to affirm the window of fertility for women and to allow women to step in and out of employment as needed to bear children *without penalty.*

Unfortunately, sequencing didn't take off. At least not in the way that encouraged women to think through the entire arc of their lives, planning ahead for seasons of intense mothering and seasons of wider community or marketplace involvement. But in its wake, the idea of "choice feminism" developed, which said that whatever choice a woman makes about directing her life is valid—including the choice to be at home full-time with children. This established the battleground of the "Mommy Wars" to come.

But in those heady, post-college days, my friends and I were more disturbed by the choices we might *not* have. In 1986, *Newsweek* published a cover story—"Too Late for Prince Charming?"—that shook a lot of young women to the core. I was one of them. *Newsweek* claimed that a forty-year-old, single, white, college-educated woman was more likely to be killed by a terrorist than to marry. Though forty seemed a long way off to me back then, I worried that this statement might actually be true.

It wasn't. Twenty years later *Newsweek* retracted it.[17]

Historian Stephanie Coontz says that the reason that this claim seemed true was because of something called the "independence effect."

> Women, the theory goes, search for mates who are good providers. But what if a woman has good earning possibilities of her own? A related theory, called the independence effect, predicts that she will have less incentive to marry, and men will also find her a less attractive mate. Moreover, if such a woman does marry, she will be more likely to divorce than other women.
>
> For centuries, the independence effect did have considerable predictive power in Western Europe and North America. Until the 1950s highly educated

women *were* less likely to marry than less educated
women.

But for women born since 1960, things are different. College graduates and women with higher
earnings are now *more* likely to marry than women
with less education and lower wages, although they
generally marry at an older age.[18]

Education and job experience also seem to stabilize marriages—
again, contrary to popular thought. After the turmoil of the women's
movement in the 1970s, the marriages of college-educated women actually became more stable in the following decades. By the mid-1990s,
college-educated American men and women under forty-five had con-
siderably lower divorce rates than those in other educational categories.[19]

The Mommy Wars

As if terrorized single women weren't enough, the 1980s still had
one more anxious concept to release upon women—and it lives on
today: the "Mommy Wars." Ostensibly fought between stay-at-home
mothers and working mothers, the "Mommy Wars" exposed the fault
lines of competitive mothering to reveal omnipresent mother guilt. No
matter what choices mothers made, it seemed someone else was always
ready to pronounce them wrong.

Perhaps the battle lives on because the children who grew up as
latchkey children in the 1980s want something different for their own
families. While writing this chapter, one of my friends told me about her
experience growing up with busy working parents. Her parents genuinely believed they were doing the right thing at the time, but Joy was
left to manage herself after school from age twelve on. Unfortunately,
she was seduced at thirteen by an older teen boy who took advantage
of her solitude. Joy's teen years were rocky ones, filled with rebellion,
deception, and self-doubt. Now she is married, the mother of three children, and a committed Christian. But she still wrestles with the basic
conflict embedded in the "Mommy Wars":

For purposes of understanding my situation,
let's assume I accept (which I do) that there is

immeasurable benefit in staying home with your children—being their primary disciplinarian, helper, caretaker, home-creator, influencer. I intend to be home with them after school until they enter college. This is because I have a strong conviction that most of my destructive choices in high school were made simply because I had no adult supervision after school, once I turned twelve. So I plan to be here, and have no plans to change that.

But here I am, six years into being a stay-at-home mother, and I find myself dying to work outside the home, to work at something that uses all my mental abilities. I wrestle with questions about calling, gifting, and fulfillment. My brain is super-active. I was a successful young entrepreneur before becoming a mom. I constantly think in money-making strategies. I love to problem solve. So slowing down to function on the level of a preschooler has been THE HARD-EST thing I have ever had to do in my life. I struggle with boredom every day. I have such a hard time pretending with them that I often turn to videos (much more than I ever intended), or to any structured activity like coloring time or room-playtime to keep them busy so that I will not be forced to "play"—which I am terrible at. Seriously, it's like a learning disability. I can't think of a thing to say when they ask me to pretend to be a bear or elephant with them. I try, but I freeze up—I yawn, my mind turns to thirty other things I could be doing (there's that e-mail to write, that meal plan to make, that family budget to update . . .). I can't stay focused on the game. Other moms have confirmed they have the same response to play time, but I think somehow I am worse. Some other moms seem more interested in the things of child-hood than I am—like my friends who have chosen home-schooling. But I feel like I am an adult, through

and through—and I don't know how to be a kid
again.

In any case, this results in a constant sense of
guilt that I carry around in all my mothering. I
should be fulfilled doing this, but I am not. I should
enjoy this playtime with my kids, but I don't. I am
not "gifted" at this full-time-playmate-for-little-kids
thing. So I do my best to take good care of them and
snuggle with them and attempt the occasional board
game, but I often feel like a failure.

Life with small kids is so sporadic and random,
it's hard to keep your home life and schedule organized perfectly. I don't know any moms who do, so
can I even hope to be great at this? What does the
Bible say mothers could be called to do in terms of
working for profit with their skills? Is it possible that
some wives and mothers, like me, *could* be called to
work more than others, or is it most likely sin if moms
want to work at things they "enjoy" more than being
focused on the home?

Women of previous generations would be surprised by Joy's idea
that a mother's role is to be a "full-time-playmate-for-little-kids." Most
cultures throughout time viewed children as an addition to the family's
productivity. The work of managing a home was too labor-intensive to
expect hours of amusement, a concept we will explore in the following
chapters.

But the questions Joy raises are valid. For all the advancements
claimed by feminism, Joy sounds a lot like the women interviewed fifty
years ago by Betty Friedan: "Is this all?" Perhaps we're not viewing the
issue from the proper perspective. Perhaps we are far more shaped by
recent history than we realize.

The End of Men?

Certainly now is the time to develop clarity about women's productivity because we are on the cusp of another profound culture shift:

More young women are getting college degrees and retaining more jobs than their male counterparts. The tipping point came in 2010 and was trumpeted in a widely-read article in the *Atlantic* titled "The End of Men":

> Earlier this year, for the first time in American his-
> tory, the balance of the workforce tipped toward
> women, who now hold a majority of the nation's jobs.
> The working class, which has long defined our notions
> of masculinity, is slowly turning into a matriarchy,
> with men increasingly absent from the home and
> women making all the decisions. Women dominate
> today's colleges and professional schools—for every
> two men who will receive a B.A. this year, three
> women will do the same. Of the 15 job categories
> projected to grow the most in the next decade in the
> U.S., all but two are occupied primarily by women.[20]

This development has profound implications for the future of the American family. While it's good that discrimination against women and unequal legal status has ended, it's not good to marginalize men. No society will benefit from pitting women against men. We need to develop better solutions.

Navigating times like these calls for a lot of wisdom. Fortunately, the Bible promises us that wisdom will be given to those who ask: "Now if any of you lacks wisdom, he should ask God, who gives to all gener-ously and without criticizing, and it will be given to him" (James 1:5). But wisdom is given to us so our lives point to the glory of God, not to ourselves. "Pay careful attention, then, to how you walk—not as unwise people but as wise—making the most of the time, because the days are evil" (Eph. 5:15–16).

Later in this book, we will look at biblical wisdom in the nature of work and explore the application of wisdom in the life cycle of work. But next we will look at the history of women's productivity from the Reformation to the Industrial Revolution, a time period when biblical concepts of work and vocation changed the Western world.

CHAPTER 3

The Back Story

The relationship that wholly changed the Western world's views of marriage, domesticity, and womanly productivity actually began with two vows of chastity.

In the midst of the restlessness of the sixteenth century, one monk and one nun entered their adult years fully expecting to live out their lives in seclusion and poverty. Katharina (Kate) von Bora entered a convent at age five and remained a nun for twenty years, until she heard the teachings of Martin Luther on biblical marriage and family. Convinced by Martin's writings, Kate secretly contacted him, requesting his help to escape. So Martin arranged a daring escape with the help of a merchant delivering herring fish—he unloaded the fish and left with the twelve nuns in his fish barrels.

Martin arranged for each of the nuns to be married or reunited with their families, until only Kate was left. She let it be known that there were only two men she would accept: Martin Luther himself or his colleague, Nikolaus von Amsdorf.

Though Martin had written much to promote Christian marriage, he had remained single because of the opposition he faced for his teaching. Challenged to practice what he preached about marriage, Martin said he remained unwed "not because I am a sexless log or stone, but because daily I expect death as a heretic."[1] However, at forty-one he decided to marry Kate because his marriage "would please his father, rile the pope, cause the angels to laugh and the devils to weep."[2]

The first challenge the new couple faced was how to support themselves. As a former nun, Kate was penniless and without a dowry. Martin had no steady income either, because the university where he taught often withheld his pay. The only income he could rely on was

the proceeds from the Black Cloister, a former monastery given to the
Luthers as a wedding present. It was up to Martin's new bride to make
the dilapidated monastery a self-sustaining home. She was more than
equal to the task, according to one biography:

> Out of bed at 4 o'clock, she was known as "Käthe
> von Bora, the Morning Star of Wittenberg." Kate was
> in good physical condition and often worked until 9
> o'clock at night. Luther often had to urge her to relax.
> Kate's first concern was the dilapidated walls of the
> former monastery. With the application of a great
> amount of lime, she whitewashed all of them. With
> the help of a maid, she then cleaned the rooms and
> put the garden in order. Luther was inspired by Kate's
> activities. He expressed his delight at the fact that "my
> wife can coax me as often as she wants; she has the
> entire dominion in her hand, and I yield to it."
>
> A careful and resourceful administrator, Kate
> used all her talents to make the Luther home self-
> supporting. Soon the Black Cloister became known
> as *Lutherhaus*. Kate became gardener, fisher, brewer,
> fruit grower, cattle and horse breeder, cook, bee-
> keeper, provisioner, nurse, and vintner. She kept on
> hand an ample supply of the vegetables and flowers
> that Luther loved. Trout, perch, and pike graced their
> table, and brews appeared for her thirsty husband and
> their guests. Pears, apples, peaches, grapes, and nuts
> were cultivated, and Kate carefully tended chickens,
> geese, pigs, cows, and work and riding horses. She
> gathered a ready supply of food to be salted for the
> winter months when fresh food would not be readily
> available.
>
> Impetus for Kate's determination to get *Lutherhaus*
> in shape and make it self-sustaining was the arrival of
> guests from all over the world. Displaced scholars, stu-
> dents, refugees, escaped nuns and monks, and several
> members of Luther's family found their way to Witten-
> berg. Thus the Luther residence became a hotel.[3]

Martin encouraged his wife's productivity. Kate was the better financial manager and, after years of his overspending, Martin agreed to rely on her business acumen. She recognized the opportunity to supplement their income by charging room and board while guests attended the famous *Lutherhaus* Table Talk gatherings. Not only was she known for her hospitality, but the table she spread became an important place where ideas were shared and disseminated. As her biographer noted, "The Luther table was one of the best news-gathering systems in the land. . . . News of the whole continent was funneled through *Lutherhaus*."⁴ Regular guests and scribes compiled approximately 6,000 entries into the records of Table Talk, leaving us with a good idea of how much work Kate undertook and how many ideas were being reshaped during this time.⁵

The marriage of Martin and Kate was also a turning point in Western history. As one historian noted, "Few people influenced the institution of marriage more than the Augustinian monk Martin Luther. . . . Luther's acceptance of children as the core of his rejuvenated life speaks for one of the Reformation's most dramatic shifts. Henceforth, the pastor's home, replete with managerial wife and children underfoot, would offer a new model for Protestant couples throughout the world."⁶ At the start of their lives, few people would have expected such a legacy from a monk and a nun. But their influence extended beyond marriage. It also changed our concept of work.

The Doctrine of Vocation

The "doctrine of vocation" is one of Martin Luther's greatest contributions to both church and culture. To Luther, vocation is more than just what you do to make a living. It is, as Gene Edward Veith writes, the theology of the Christian life:

> It solves the much-vexed problems of the relationship
> between faith and works, Christ and culture, how
> Christians are to live in the world. . . . According to
> Luther, vocation is a "mask of God." He is hidden in
> vocation. We see the milkmaid, or the farmer, or the
> doctor or pastor or artist. But, looming behind this

human mask, God is genuinely present and active
in what they do for us. When we pray the Lord's
Prayer, we ask God to give us this day our daily bread.
And he does. The way he gives us our daily bread is
through the vocations of farmers, millers, and bakers.
We might add truck drivers, factory workers, bankers,
warehouse attendants, and the lady at the checkout
counter. Virtually every step of our whole economic
system contributes to that piece of toast you had for
breakfast. And when you thanked God for the food
that he provided, you were right to do so.[7]

In the monastic world of Luther's early life, holiness and salvation
were obtained by "good works"—which meant removing oneself from
the sinful world to embrace celibacy, poverty, and the daily practice of
specific spiritual exercises. But, as Veith writes, Luther denied the value
of this practice: "He would ask, Who are you helping? Good works are
not to be done for God. Rather, they must be done for one's neighbor."[8]

Luther understood vocation to mean multiple realms of service. The
work of family, in Luther's view, not only included marriage and children, but also the labor by which households make their livings. "Luther
had in mind what is expressed in the Greek word *oikonomia*, referring to
'the management and the regulation of the resources of the household,'
the term from which we derive our word economy," Veith writes. "Thus,
the estate of the household includes both the family vocations and the
vocations of the workplace."[9]

Perhaps watching his wife work so hard convinced Martin of this
concept. Kate was an early entrepreneur in the classic "Protestant work
ethic" that arose from her husband's teachings on vocation. By affirm-
ing the daily labors of men and women outside of the church, Luther
inspired men and women alike to engage in trade, develop their own
enterprises, and work hard for the benefit of strangers. This idea inspired
the rise of capitalism and the economic gains that would follow in sub-
sequent eras.

Motherhood

Luther, Sarah Edwards was a hard worker. She lived in colonial America during the early 1700s as the wife of Jonathan Edwards, one of America's greatest theologians and intellectuals. Settled by mostly Protestant Christians, colonial America was a showcase for the Protestant work ethic. Sarah managed their household economy so well that Jonathan was able to concentrate on his writing and teaching, which became a significant influence in the first major revival of colonial America, the Great Awakening.

The legendary story about their relationship is that one day Jonathan looked up from his study in their Northampton, Massachusetts, home and inquired, "Isn't it about time the hay was cut?" To which Sarah responded, "It's been in the barn for two weeks."[10]

It's quite unlikely Sarah cut any of that hay herself, especially as she was busy with their eleven children. But she was managing the property that came with Jonathan's position as a minister: 10 acres of pasture, 40 acres of meadow, and 10 additional acres on a hill, as well as the £300 toward his housing and £100 a year as salary, which came out of the local taxes.[11] The land had to provide for their own consumption, as well as for the numerous guests who always turned up for Sarah's legendary hospitality. Like the *Lutherhaus* before them, the Edwards' home attracted many young men who wanted to learn from Jonathan in person. Their guests were part of the family business, so to speak, but their presence required more than extra food. Sarah also had to make the household soap, candles, and homegrown wool for clothing and bedding. All this she did with a preoccupied husband who often skipped meals because he was too deep in his studies. Sarah's household administration enabled her husband to spend thirteen hours a day in his study[12]—creating a rich legacy of ideas for the culture of the time and the believers who came after him.

The Edwards family lived like most of colonial America—working hard at a variety of tasks, but never far apart from each other. As historian Nancy Pearcey points out, fathers and mothers alike merged their work and childrearing responsibilities into the daily activities of that time. Fathers trained their children to work alongside them and they were quite involved as parents:

Being a father was not a separate activity to come
home to after a day at work; rather, it was an integral
part of a man's daily routine. Historical records reveal
that colonial literature on parenting—like sermons
and child-rearing manuals—were not addressed to
mothers, as the majority are today. Instead, they were
typically addressed to fathers. Fathers were considered
the primary parent, and were held to be particularly
important in their children's religious and intellectual
training.[13]

There was also no thought at this time that the home was a separate
sphere from "real" life. The home was the economic base of the local
community, and the local community flowed in and out of the home:

Work was not done by lone individuals but by families or households. A household was a relatively auton-
omous economic unit often including members of
the extended family, apprentices, servants, and hired
hands. Stores, offices, and workshops were located in
a front room, with living quarters either upstairs or in
the rear. This meant that the boundary between home
and world was highly permeable: The "world" entered
continually in the form of clients, business colleagues,
customers, and apprentices.[14]

While much of the labor in colonial America was focused on simple
survival, by the time of the American Revolution, the consumer choices
that these women made took on political overtones. To protest the
imposition of taxes without representation, they boycotted items such as
British tea and cloth. This was no light decision, either. Without British
cloth, American women had to return to spinning and weaving their
own cloth—skills that had fallen into disuse, according to the author of
Revolutionary Mothers:

"Cloths of your own make and spinning," or home-
spun, quickly became a badge of honor and a visible political statement. . . . Urged by the press, by
ministers, and by the colonial leadership to look upon

domestic duties and chores as political weapons, these
women began to see themselves, for the first time, as
actors upon the political stage.[15]

After the United States of America was founded, the rest of the
world looked upon this upstart nation with its democratic values and
wondered if it would succeed. So did many of the founding fathers.
In fact, it wasn't long before political leaders realized that if this grand
political experiment were to work, it would need a new generation of
public-spirited citizens. Therefore, American mothers were enlisted in
the important goal of training the next generation of Americans. This
was called "Republican Motherhood." Not the red state/blue state kind,
but a wholehearted embrace of the importance of educated mothers
training future citizens for this new republic of the United States. As
a result, female literacy shot up shortly after the nation was founded.[16]

The Industrial Revolution

While the colonies were fighting the American Revolution, Britain
was in the throes of the Industrial Revolution. It took a little longer
for this revolution to reach the United States. Historians often peg
the beginning of the American Industrial Revolution to when the first
industrial mill opened in 1790 in Rhode Island. But when it arrived,
the Industrial Revolution profoundly transformed American life and
families.

For the first time in history, work was being done on a mass scale
outside of the home or family business. As more men were hired to work
in factories and offices and encouraged to be competitive in the world
of manufacturing and business, women promoted the "haven of home"
as a counter-balance. This is when the idea of "separate spheres" arose,
appointing women to the domestic sphere and the cultivation of virtues
private and public and men to the public sphere as wage-earners. Thus,
as the workplace became increasingly mechanized and impersonal, the
home became the focus for the intangible qualities that improved society. This time period, spanning roughly 1830 to 1850, became known
as the Golden Age of Domesticity.

This ideal dominated the women's magazines and books of the day, but it was attainable only for wealthy, upper class women. For women of lower economic status, the Industrial Revolution drew many girls from family farms or enterprises to become wage earners at a factory or mill, offering them a form of independence they had not experienced before.

In 1826, just as the Golden Age of Domesticity was taking off, thousands of New England farm girls were recruited to operate the textile mills in the new town of Lowell, Massachusetts. Lowell was created in 1826 by a group of Boston capitalists who bought the farms along the Merrimack River to power the mills. Less than twenty years later, the Lowell mills employed nearly 8,000 women between the ages of sixteen and thirty-five. Lowell Mill Girls, as they came to be called, worked very hard, averaging more than seventy hours per week.

They were also very profitable workers, which stimulated more mill construction. This rapid expansion, unfortunately, led to over-production, deflated prices, and, thus, lower wages for the workers. It only took ten years for the Lowell Mill Girls to be the first ones to organize a strike. Harriet Hanson Robinson was one of those Lowell Mill Girls; she began work there at the age of ten. In her memoir, she wrote about the strike of 1836:

> One of the first strikes of cotton-factory operatives
> that ever took place in this country was that in Low-
> ell, in October 1836. When it was announced that the
> wages were to be cut down, great indignation was felt,
> and it was decided to strike, en masse. This was done.
> The mills were shut down, and the girls went in pro-
> cession from their several corporations to the "grove"
> on Chapel Hill, and listened to "incendiary" speeches
> from early labor reformers.
>
> One of the girls stood on a pump, and gave vent
> to the feelings of her companions in a neat speech,
> declaring that it was their duty to resist all attempts
> at cutting down the wages. This was the first time
> a woman had spoken in public in Lowell, and the
> event caused surprise and consternation among her
> audience.

> It is hardly necessary to say that so far as results
> were concerned this strike did no good. The dissatis-
> faction of the operatives subsided, or burned itself out,
> and though the authorities did not accede to their
> demands, the majority returned to their work, and the
> corporation went on cutting down the wages.[17]

The conditions in the mills were grim by current work standards, but the attraction of working there was the opportunity for self-improvement. Lowell offered opportunities for further education through courses and public lectures, as well as its informal literary circles. But these opportunities dwindled as wages were reduced and the pace of work within the mills was stepped up. In 1845, after a number of protests and strikes, many of the workers came together to form the first union of working women in the United States, the Lowell Female Labor Reform Association.

"In an era in which women had to overcome opposition simply to work in the mills, it is remarkable that they would further overstep the accepted middle-class bounds of female propriety by participating in a public protest," one historian writes. "The experiences of Lowell women before 1850 present a fascinating picture of the contradictory impact of industrial capitalism. . . . The Lowell mills both exploited and liberated women in ways unknown to the preindustrial political economy."[18]

Fervent Ideals, New Opportunities

The Lowell Mill Girls framed their arguments for reform in the spirit of the American Revolution. That was typical of the nineteenth century. It was a time of fervent ideals politically, culturally, and spiritually—ideals that shaped the way women worked in the home and outside of it.

The century began as the Second Great Awakening (1790–1840) swept the nation, attracting more women than men. By one estimate, there were at least three females to every two males converted in these revivals.[19] This revival inspired the first American missionary movement and created a new occupation for women—missionaries. In 1810, the American Board of Commissioners for Foreign Missions (ABCFM) was formed and became the leading missionary society in the United States. In 1812, the ABCFM sent its first missionaries to British India, a group of men and women that included Adoniram and Ann Judson. Less than ten years later, the missionary organization commissioned Ellen Stetson, the first unmarried female missionary, and Betsey Stockton, the first African-American missionary.[20]

Using the moral authority of the housewife derived from the Golden Age of Domesticity, women also used their literary gifts to transform society. Author Harriet Beecher Stowe is one of the best examples, as she challenged the nation with her anti-slavery views in the 1852 publication of *Uncle Tom's Cabin*. She was a preacher's daughter, "living on the edge of genteel poverty," who wrote the first masterpiece of American realism, a remarkable feat according to historian Glenna Matthews:

> First, American novelists had been—almost to a person—silent on the subject of slavery up to 1851. Second, although women writers were tapping a vast market with the domestic novel, there were few attempting to write on public issues for a general audience. . . . Finally, Stowe, though the member of an accomplished family, had no reason to think of herself as destined for a public role. Her life had been difficult . . . because her husband Calvin was never able to provide more than the barest necessities for his family, and Stowe's own writing did not yet provide enough revenue to supply the lack.[21]

Her writing and its strong Christian message was initially serialized in the *National Era* and later published in book form by 1852. Less than a year later, more than 300,000 copies had sold and the nation's conscience was torn on the issue of slavery. During the Civil War, when Abraham Lincoln finally met Harriet, he was reported to say, "So, you're the little lady who started this big war."[22]

There were several "little ladies" during this time whose fervent ideals also changed the society around them and created new job opportunities for women. Dorothea Dix was a crusader throughout the 1840s for mental health reforms, lobbying for the first generation of American mental asylums. (Though we might think differently about asylums in this era, in Dorothea's day, the poor who suffered mental illness were confined like caged animals or worse.) Her work among mentally ill patients led to her appointment as the Superintendent of Army Nurses during the Civil War.

Florence Nightingale is credited with revolutionizing nursing world-wide, establishing standards of care and professional training in a field that had largely been seen as a disreputable profession. Until Nightingale organized field hospitals during the Crimean War (1853–56), no woman had ever before served as a battle nurse. Clara Barton followed her exam-ple in the Civil War and later founded the American Red Cross. In an era when the term "female physician" meant abortionist, Elizabeth Blackwell became the first American woman to graduate from medical school. She attended Geneva College in New York after she was rejected by all the major medical schools in the nation because of her sex. She later founded a women's medical college to train other women physicians.

Women served the church with their labors, as well. One of the more prolific writers of the nineteenth century was the hymn writer Fanny Crosby. She wrote more than 8,000 hymns and religious poems, even though she had been blind since infancy. At one point, she was under contract to write three hymns a week, but could churn out up to six or seven hymns a day. Her work influenced her outreach, as well. Fanny taught for twenty-three years at the New York School for the Blind and lived in the tenement buildings of New York so that she could minister to the poor. She kept a very full schedule, even into her eighties.

As the Industrial Revolution continued to reshape the working lives of women, one British minister, John Angell James, wrote a guide to female piety during this time and acknowledged the realities of those who worked outside the home: "You should never allow yourselves for a moment to imagine that there is anything dishonorable or degrading in your being compelled to leave home and to support yourself, either as a governess, shopwoman, or servant. Those who have been in better cir-cumstances are, of course, most apt to feel this. . . . Industry is far more honorable than wealthy indolence; and she who willingly, honestly, and cheerfully earns her own support, when Providence has deprived her of her patrimony, is far more to be admired than she would have been had she throughout life rolled in her father's affluence, and been surrounded by every luxury."[23]

Turning Points

The fervent ideals that had created so much optimism in the early part of the nineteenth century were challenged by two upheavals that arrived near the middle of the century. The first was the 1859 publication of Charles Darwin's theory of evolution, which influenced the ideas of Social Darwinism. The second was the American Civil War (1861–65) and the emancipation of former slaves that followed.

Social Darwinism reversed the status of the home as the moral center of culture that had been promoted during the previous decades. As historian Nancy Pearcey writes, "Social Darwinism took direct aim on the home by exalting the public sphere as the seat of evolutionary progress." She adds:

> Beginning with the assumption that men are superior to women, Social Darwinists like Herbert Spencer sought to explain why men had evolved faster. They proposed that, from their brute beginnings, males fought for survival out in the world and were thus subject to natural selection, a process that weeds out the weak and inferior. Women, at home nurturing the young, were out of reach of natural selection and hence evolved more slowly. What is significant is the contempt Social Darwinists expressed for both women's character and women's environment (i.e., the home). Home life was denounced as a drag on evolutionary development.[24]

The domestic sphere had also taken a hit because single women realized their limitations if they married. By 1860, as the Golden Age of Domesticity was coming to a close, single working women represented one quarter of the total U.S. workforce.[25] Under the legal concept of *coverture*, if they married, adult women were not an independent legal entity. Women were subsumed into the identity of their husbands, not allowed to own property, sign contracts, or earn their own salaries—and any wages were required to be relinquished to their husbands. This was the era of "single blessedness" as single women often chose their causes over the institution of marriage that existed under *coverture*. Though these laws were gradually changed in the second half of the nineteenth century, from the 1870s to around 1913, the marriage rate among educated women plunged to 60 percent (as compared to 90 percent in the general population).[26] But personal choice wasn't the only reason for a growing number of unmarried women. The Civil War also created a major gender imbalance as more than 600,000 men died during the war, mostly from the South, sending unmarried women out in droves searching for work.

Emancipation for previously enslaved women was another upheaval in the middle of the nineteenth century, depleting the South of unpaid labor in its cotton fields and homes, and providing the North with much-needed cheap labor for its factories. Achieving freedom for enslaved people and winning the war dominated the strategic thinking of that time, leaving little forethought about what would happen afterward. As one historian wrote: "Little if any thought was given to what would happen to black people after emancipation. Questions about where they would go, what they would eat, how they would work and, most important, how they would survive the war were not considered, either by policy makers in Washington or the majority of generals in the field."[27]

These issues—and the drive for women's suffrage (the right to vote)—shaped the second half of the nineteenth century. In the spirit of Republican Motherhood, public education became compulsory in the 1860s. Women's colleges were also established: Vassar (1861), Wellesley (1870), Smith (1871) and Bryn Mawr (1885), among them. Between 1890 and 1910, the number of women attending college tripled.[28] As education became increasingly important, it created new jobs for women; by 1910, 98 percent of all teachers in the public-school system were women.[29]

Christian women were equally as committed to the cause of education, but for more spiritual reasons. For the thirty years following the start of the Civil War, women established both foreign and home missionary societies. Women were the first to organize missionary training schools, where students attended for one or two years to learn the Bible, the history of missions, and practical elements of urban reform. By 1909, the women's missionary boards had "6,000 Bible women and native helpers, as well as 800 teachers, 140 physicians, 79 nurses, and

380 evangelists" on the mission field at one time. One decade later, there were three million women working in missionary societies—outpacing every other type of women's organizations.[30]

But the industrious optimism of the nineteenth century would not last.

A New Century

With the publication of his 1899 book, *Theory of the Leisure Class*, economist Thorstein Veblen captured the tone of the new century. He coined the term "conspicuous consumption," and said that the lack of paid employment for the middle-class wife was a sign of her husband's social status. In this new era of consumerism, married women were targeted as buyers of items intended to showcase the family's income status.[31]

By the time of the Roaring Twenties, a majority of American children lived in families where the husband was the primary wage earner, the wife was not employed full-time outside the home or in the family enterprise, and the children themselves were in school instead of at work. This was a new pattern for American families. One reason for this was that families could afford this structure—men's wages rose dramatically in the unprecedented prosperity of the 1920s. Another reason was that job segregation and pay discrimination against women had actually *increased* during the first four decades of the twentieth century.[32]

Then came the 1929 stock market crash and the Great Depression of the 1930s. The economic fallout was staggering across North America and Europe. In desperation, married women took any job they could find. Though less than six percent of American wives worked outside the home in 1900, by the mid-1930s that figure had more than doubled. But married or single, women faced great hostility if they held jobs during the Depression. So many people were struggling financially that a working woman was seen as stealing a job from a man and undermining his ability to provide for his family. That attitude was so prevalent that by 1932, the U.S. Economy Act prohibited the federal government from employing two people from the same family and 26 states had passed legislation prohibiting married women from holding any jobs at all, including teaching.[33]

One year into the next decade, everything boomeranged. As we saw in the previous chapter, with the start of World War II, women were back in favor as the Office of War Information churned out working-girl propaganda. For the first time in U.S. history, there were more married than single women in the labor force.[34]

A Place of Consumption

Kate Luther and Sarah Edwards no doubt would have a hard time understanding the fractured family as it exists now, with everyone in the household pulled in different directions. Though these women worked very hard, their daily tasks were closely aligned with that of their husbands and children. The frenetic schedule of today's family would seem odd in comparison.

The Industrial Revolution generated immense wealth and created a large middle class of prosperous professionals that had never existed before. But it also divided the daily lives of men and women, negatively impacting the influence of the home where women had traditionally been economically productive.

When the American home became a showcase for consumption, it altered centuries of productivity and introduced a number of present challenges. First, the home had stopped being a place that generated income. Though it was good that new occupations had opened for women outside of the home, now they had to figure out how to rear a family and provide for themselves while working in different locations.

Second, in the process of demeaning domesticity, the culture neglects to validate the significance of the work done in the home to care for others. The private sphere remains a place where unpaid work has eternal merit. In accepting the culture of consumerism, homes become a monument to personal style and taste, rather than places of service to others. These days the "new domesticity" popularized on blogs and social media sites is wildly popular; and it brings with it the same aspirations about productivity idealized in those glossy ads of the 1950s. It sells a lifestyle. Now Nora and I confess a certain weakness ourselves for being domestic divas—aprons and all—but we don't believe it ends with a fabulous meal. It's about feeding souls, providing a refuge for the weary, and living generously.

Women like Sarah Edwards and Kate Luther understood knew that work has a bigger scope. It wasn't just about their efficiency or effectiveness on the job; sometimes it was about making others a success too.

Dozens of pages about Western history show we are still ill-equipped to solve our own challenges. Love and labor, home and work—these concepts need an eternal perspective. That's why, in the next chapter, we will go back even further in history, to understand the context of work found in the Ancient Story.

CHAPTER 4

The Ancient Story

It's called "the reveal."

In the television industry, that's the term for the moment when the makeover—of home or person—is shown to an admiring throng of people whose sole reason for existence at that moment is to squeal, cry, and clap their hands over their mouths in shock. Preferably, all three at once.

As the curtain is pulled back, the "reveal" can shape how you think about your own choices. You may think about your home's style or, if you are honest, you may think about *that* room, the one with the expanding piles of procrastination. With the dozens and dozens of magazines, cable shows, and Pinterest boards, it's no surprise if you think about your home as an expression of your identity.

As we saw in the previous chapter, that's not the concept of the home that most people have had throughout history. The home was a center of productivity. If we don't know that history, then we will read the biblical verses about the home only through the lens of our current experience—and potentially misunderstand the intent of these passages.

Consider two such verses from the New Testament:

> But refuse to enroll younger widows, for when their passions draw them away from Christ, they desire to marry and so incur condemnation for having abandoned their former faith. Besides that, they learn to be idlers, going about from house to house, and not only idlers, but also gossips and busybodies, saying what they should not. So I would have younger widows marry, bear children, *manage their households*, and give

the adversary no occasion for slander. (1 Tim. 5:11–14 ESV, emphasis added)

> Older women likewise are to be reverent in behavior, not slanderers or slaves to much wine. They are to teach what is good, and so train the young women to love their husbands and children, to be self-controlled, pure, *working at home,* kind, and submissive to their own husbands, that the word of God may not be reviled. (Titus 2:3–5 ESV, emphasis added)

Both of these passages were written by the apostle Paul, who has been accused in certain circles of being oppressively sexist because of what he writes about women. But if you correctly understand the experiences of the first-century church, its Jewish heritage, and the Roman culture surrounding it, Paul is actually rather progressive.

Over the last several centuries, Christians have engaged in this debate about where women should be productive. When mainstream culture devalued marriage and motherhood, Christians (and those from some other faith traditions) rightly upheld these important roles. When mainstream culture overvalued the workplace, they also rightly upheld the value of the home.

The only problem is that our modern concept of the home is not the same as the biblical concept. As we saw in the last chapter, for most of human history, the home was the original small business unit, the building block of a community's economic vitality. It was only after the upheaval of the Industrial Revolution that the home moved from being a place of productivity to a place of consumption.

For Paul to counsel women to manage their households and work at home was to say women's work is important in both the physical and the spiritual realms. He was not limiting the scope of work for women today. We cannot accuse Paul of being sexist when he recommended women manage their homes. As we will see, he was being *strategic.*

So instead of a modern makeover with the big "reveal," let's pull back the curtain on an ancient story instead. We are going to learn from the examples of two women in Scripture by digging in to understand their stories and culture. That will help us to then apply the timeless commands from the Bible that always transcend culture.

The Color Purple

When Paul wrote those two commands we cited earlier, he was writing to younger pastors named Timothy and Titus. He was addressing both the specific issues that they faced in their churches and the larger picture of how Christ-followers were to live. If we don't consider both angles, we can miss some important points. As historian and theologian Bruce Winter notes, the theological preconceptions attributed to Paul have been thoroughly examined, but little attention has been given to the actual setting of the women under discussion.[1]

So let's start with a tradeswoman named Lydia. We find her story in Acts 16. Paul had just arrived in Philippi, a Roman colony and a leading city in the Greek province of Macedonia.

> On the Sabbath day we went outside the city gate by the river, where we thought there was a place of prayer. We sat down and spoke to the women gathered there. A woman named Lydia, a dealer in purple cloth from the city of Thyatira, who worshiped God, was listening. The Lord opened her heart to pay attention to what was spoken by Paul. After she and her household were baptized, she urged us, "If you consider me a believer in the Lord, come and stay at my house." And she persuaded us. (Acts 16:13–15)

Just a few verses earlier, we are told that Paul's ambition to evangelize Asia Minor was thwarted by the clear direction of the Holy Spirit. In response to a dream in which a Macedonian man pleads for him to visit, Paul goes to Philippi, a leading city of the Macedonian region, now part of modern Greece. There he meets a woman who will become his first European convert. But she is not from Philippi. Her hometown of Thyatira was actually in the very region in Asia Minor that Paul was prevented by the Holy Spirit to visit. "The ironies are many," writes Bible teacher John MacArthur:

Instead of reaching Lydia in the region she regarded as home, the gospel pursued her to Europe, where she was engaged in business. Although Paul saw a Macedonian man in his vision, an Asian woman became the first convert on record in Europe.[2]

Because she sold purple dye and fancy purple cloth, it was likely that Lydia's profession led her to Europe. This dye was the basis for the official royal purple, which made that substance one of the most precious of all commodities in the ancient world. Her business was likely very profitable.[3]

Lydia's first response to hearing the gospel is to offer hospitality to Paul and his traveling companions. Her home eventually became the base for the new church in Philippi—the first church in Europe. Lydia's marital status is uncertain; but what we do know is that she was a wealthy woman who ran a large and productive home, likely staffed by a number of household bondservants or slaves. (This is not comparable to American slavery. Roman slaves had no identifying marks, they could dress as freemen, they could buy their freedom, and some could eventually become Roman citizens.)[4] As MacArthur points out, Paul had no immediate plans for his future, so Lydia's offer was to keep them indefinitely:

> The real cost to Lydia was potentially much higher than the monetary value of room and board for a group of missionaries. Remember that Philippi was where Paul and Silas were beaten badly, thrown in jail, and clamped to stocks. They were ultimately freed by a miraculous earthquake, and the jailer and all his household became Christians in the process. But if preaching the gospel was deemed a jailable offense, Lydia was exposing herself to possible trouble—a loss of business, bad will in the community, and even a prison sentence for herself—by housing these strangers and thus giving them a base from which to evangelize.[5]

Lydia's profitable work enabled her to be a bold partner in the gospel to Paul and his missionary companions and a patron of the new church begun in Philippi. In this, she followed in the footsteps of Susanna, Joanna, and Mary Magdalene, women who supported Jesus and His disciples "out of their own means" (Luke 8:3 NIV).

The New Woman

If Paul was willing to be supported by a tradeswoman like Lydia, why would he recommend women to be busy at home, managing their households? First, as we've already seen, most jobs at that time were based in or near the home. If today we read those passages through our own cultural context, and assume Paul wanted women sidelined and not in a place of influence, it would benefit us to look closer at the cultural context of Paul's time. By doing so, we will see that's exactly the *opposite* of what Paul meant. He wanted women to be influential and strategic for the sake of the gospel.

At the time Lydia was converted, elite women were rebelling against the sexual double standard in Roman families. A few decades earlier, during the reign of Caesar Augustus (27 BC to AD 14), some Roman wives began to pursue the same sexual immorality as their husbands, joining them in debauched dinners and drinking parties, and pursuing younger men. This pattern was later called the "new woman."

Not surprisingly, marriage rates fell, birth rates fell, and abortion was not uncommon. Concerned about the welfare of the empire, Augustus rolled out social legislation to combat these trends, a set of laws generally known as the *lex Julia*, written around 17 BC. These laws regulated marriage and sexual activities, provided legal and financial incentives for having children, enacted penalties for refusing to do so, and issued laws surrounding adultery and divorce. For example, husbands were forbidden from "honor killings" if they discovered their wives with another man, but they were also required to initiate legal action within sixty days to initiate divorce and a trial for adultery. If that wasn't done promptly, such a husband was open to the charge of "pimping" his wife. Wives convicted of adultery faced even more severe penalties. "Once divorced and found guilty of adultery by a court, the wife lost half of her dowry, one third of any other property she owned, and was relegated to an island," Winter writes. "A woman so convicted could not thereafter enter into a fully valid marriage."[6]

These new laws attempted to create two classes of women—the virtuous and the promiscuous. This class division was signaled through clothing, because in Roman jurisprudence, you were what you wore. In 28 BC, Caesar Augustus legislated the kind of clothing that could be worn by married women, convicted adulterous wives, and prostitutes. Married women were to wear the *stola* (a large sleeveless overgarment suspended from the shoulders) and *vittae* (a hairband), items that were legally forbidden to prostitutes. While Roman men wore the toga, the only women who were to wear the toga were women convicted of adultery, and they were to wear it as a symbol of their shame.

These laws also forbid women descended from, or married to, elite classes from becoming the high-class prostitutes known as courtesans or *hetairai*. The *hetairai* dressed lavishly with much jewelry and sometimes even wore transparent clothing, in stark contrast to the matrons with their veils and *stola*.

Most unfortunately for Augustus, his own daughter—ironically named Julia—would not comply with the *lex Julia* regulations and was tried for adultery in 2 BC. The Roman writer Seneca noted that Augustus was "'alarmed by his daughter and the noble youths who were bound to her by adultery as if by a military oath.' He complained that 'she received lovers in droves . . . roamed the city in nocturnal revels. . . . Turning from adultery to prostitution . . . [she sought] gratification of every kind in the arms of casual lovers.'"[7]

Like Julia, many elite women rebelled against these new laws. Though married, some acted like the *hetairai* and even officially registered as prostitutes because the adultery laws did not apply to that class of society. But Augustus continued his campaign, calling both men and women to a higher standard of conduct for the sake of the Empire. In an assembly of bachelors, Augustus said there was no better relationship than a marriage where "a wife is of chaste conduct . . . domestic, mistress of the house, its good stewardess, a rearer of children; one . . . to restrain the mad passion of youth."[8]

Augustus saw how important these virtues were to a stable society. But unfortunately this promiscuity continued, luring women away from the responsibilities of running a complex household. This was the culture to which Paul ministered as he traveled throughout the Roman Empire, and it bears many similarities to our culture today. But Paul came with a message that transcended the agenda of Augustus and it is what we need to hear, as well.

Advancing the Gospel

The apostle Paul was formerly a Pharisee and a rabbi. As such, he grew up in a world where men and women were highly segregated. Women were restricted in the temple to the outer court of the women and sat apart from men in synagogues. Jewish rabbis did not even make eye contact with women who were not family members, much less speak to them. It's likely that he prayed the daily Jewish prayer thanking God he was made a man and not a woman, slave, or Gentile.

Yet after conversion, he referred to women as his fellow contenders for the gospel (Phil. 4:1–3). He commended Phoebe as a deacon and a patron (Rom. 16:1–2). He labored and evangelized with a married couple, Priscilla and Aquila (vv. 3–4). Instead of his former prayers thanking God he was not born a woman, a slave, or a Gentile, Paul penned Galatians 3:28: "There is no Jew or Greek, slave or free, male or female; for you are all one in Christ Jesus."

Remember that Paul wrote his letters as a Roman citizen, which meant he was no doubt aware of the culture and the laws and the way they shaped the culture he was trying to reach—he knew what was affecting marriage and family. But amid these Roman laws, and the Jewish practices that allowed a man to divorce his wife almost at will, Paul upheld a different standard: the words of Jesus. Against a sexually permissive culture, Paul did not condone divorce or promiscuity for either men or women. Against the common practice of sexual immorality and promiscuity, Paul urged self-control for everyone—mentioned specifically each time for older men, older women, younger men and younger women (Titus 2).

Unlike Augustus, Paul was not concerned with the welfare of the State. His allegiance was to a greater kingdom; therefore he urged Christians to behave in such a way "so that in everything they may adorn the doctrine of God our Savior" (Titus 2:10 ESV). As historian Diana Severance notes:

The apostles did not accommodate their instruction to the culture, but enjoined Christians in their personal relations to live out their new life in Christ. Paul told wives "to submit to your own husbands as to the Lord;" Peter told them to accept their husband's authority. Husbands were told to "love your wives and do not be harsh with them," to "love your wives just as Christ loved the church," and to "live with your wives in an understanding way, showing honor to the woman." Nothing like these commands could be found in any Greco-Roman household management manuals. Paul and Peter were not just trying to maintain the social order. They were showing how Christians should live and ultimately transform the social order. The attitudes and behaviors of both husband and wife were to be molded by their relationship with Christ.[9]

Paul was countercultural in his views of women. Not only did he encourage women to be productive in a culture that made the most of pleasure, he affirmed them. Paul affirmed women in how their work glorified God. He saw the labor of women in their homes—perhaps through the example of Lydia—as a strategic rebuttal to the slander of the Enemy. Lydia was a woman who used everything she had—her influence, home, relationships, money, and even her work—to further the advance of the gospel. Perhaps that's what came to Paul's mind when he instructed Timothy and Titus to counsel women to shun gossipy idleness and instead, get back to work managing their households.

An Archetype of Wisdom

The New Testament's commendation of industrious women flows out of the ideas of female productivity in the Old Testament. The best-known example is the woman of Proverbs 31. Hers is the last story we will examine in this narrative about work.

The most important thing you need to know about this Old Testament "superwoman" is that she never existed. Found at the conclusion of the Old Testament's book of wisdom, she is only an archetype of what an excellent woman looks like, a compilation of fruitful activity in various seasons of life.

She is described in Proverbs 31:10–31, in an acrostic of verses about female excellence, one for each letter of the Hebrew alphabet. They are the sayings of an unknown king, taught to him by his mother. Presumably this mother was multitasking—teaching her son both his alphabet and the characteristics of a woman who would make an excellent wife.

Though we might think we know the Proverbs 31 woman well, once again we need to dust off our notions of her and examine this tribute closely to "reveal" what we can learn from her. This poetic tribute is a jumble of feminine qualities—addressing relationships, productivity, fruitfulness, and financial savvy—with only one short verse about beauty. It's easy to overlook the fact that this chapter has a lot more to say about her work than anything else.

Let's break it down, verse by verse:

> An excellent wife who can find? She is far more precious than jewels. (v. 10 esv)

This verse has a lot of nuance packed in it. The HCSB translates this Hebrew phrase as a "capable wife." The original NIV translates it as "a wife of noble character." This excellent, capable, noble woman is highly regarded because of how she invests these talents and skills for the betterment of everyone around her.

> The heart of her husband trusts in her, and he will
> have no lack of gain. She does him good, and not
> harm, all the days of her life. (vv. 11–12 esv)

Some today might wince that such a woman is described in her role as a wife, but that was not the Hebrew mind-set. Unlike American individualism, most cultures historically (and many even now) think more in terms of community identity. As theologian Barry Danylak writes, marriage and procreation were fundamental to Israelite society:

> Beyond being fundamental markers of God's
> covenantal blessing, marriage and offspring were

vital in Israelite society in two other respects. First,
marriage and offspring were necessary for retaining
one's inheritance of allocated land within the family.
Second, offspring and the land were necessary for
preserving one's name after death. To have no offspring resulted in losing one's land and consequently
having one's name blotted from remembrance within
the clan and the nation—a fate worse than physical
death itself. . . . In short, marriage was the universal
practice in ancient Israel because to be married and
have offspring was evidence of God's blessing *and* by
implication evidence of faithfulness to the covenant.[10]

Though this portrait highlights a married woman, single readers should remember that Jesus is the fulfillment of God's covenantal
blessing for all of us. He gives us His full and complete righteousness
in exchange for our sin and barrenness, and then gives us His name
and inheritance. The tribute to marriage is not meant to exclude single
women, rather to highlight characteristics for all women to strive to
embody.

In that setting, this acrostic poem outlines what a fruitful and productive woman looks like in a variety of ways:

> She selects wool and flax and works with willing
> hands. She is like the merchant ships, bringing her
> food from far away. She rises while it is still night and
> provides food for her household and portions for her
> female servants. She evaluates a field and buys it; she
> plants a vineyard with her earnings. She draws on her
> strength and reveals that her arms are strong. She sees
> that her profits are good, and her lamp never goes out
> at night. She extends her hands to the spinning staff,
> and her hands hold the spindle. (vv. 13–19 ESV)

The key to all of this is that this woman "works with willing hands."
She does not see her obligations as a burden. She delights in the work she
is given. Moreover, she is enterprising, energetic, strong, and hospitable

in those tasks. She sees that "her profits are good," which literally means she "tastes" or savors the fruit of her achievements.

Her primary responsibilities were to provide food and clothing for her household. That was no small task in the ancient world. These duties had become the work that women performed because the tasks were compatible with childcare. As one historian writes, "Just such are the crafts of spinning, weaving, and sewing: repetitive, easy to pick up at any point, reasonably child-safe, and easily done at home. . . . The only other occupation that fits the criteria even half so well is that of preparing the daily food. Food and clothing: These are what societies worldwide have come to see as the core of women's work (although other tasks may be added to the load, depending upon the circumstances of the particular society)."[11]

For centuries, women used a spindle to twist raw fiber into thread, until the Middle Ages, when the spinning wheel was invented, which allowed women to spin about four times faster than by hand. This work wasn't difficult, but it required consistent and constant application to supply enough thread for the needs of the household and the trading community.

That is why the wise Proverbs 31 woman is also heralded as an effective manager. The *ESV Study Bible* says that "by providing for her household and her maidens before the day begins, the 'excellent wife' multiplies the effectiveness of her work, because her planning enables everyone else in her household to be productive throughout the day."[12]

Her planning is not for just the foreseeable future, however. This woman thinks long-term. She trades profitably so that she has earnings, and then she multiplies those earnings by buying a field and planting a vineyard—a long-term investment. Even today it takes a good three years or more for a vine to mature and produce fruit. This wise woman is strategic about investing in the future, thinking ahead to what the next season might bring and how to prepare for it.

> Her hands reach out to the poor, and she extends her
> hands to the needy. (v. 20)

While she runs a busy household and a small business, this woman is never too busy to help the unfortunate. Her productivity is not an excuse for overlooking other people's needs. This woman of noble character is strong, and her strong arms bear up the weak and needy. She takes the initiative and offers a personal touch to the needy.

> She is not afraid for her household when it snows, for all in her household are doubly clothed. She makes her own bed coverings; her clothing is fine linen and purple. . . . She makes and sells linen garments; she delivers belts to the merchants. (vv. 21–22; 24)

Once again, we see how this woman plans ahead—even for events that rarely occur in her climate, such as snow. She anticipates the changing of the seasons and has prepared enough clothing to keep her household warm. Furthermore, this verse reveals that she is a skilled artisan. A sheet of fine linen was a true luxury and shows her skill as she worked with flax. The purple clothing in this context shows how prosperous such a family would be.

> Her husband is known in the gates when he sits among the elders of the land. (v. 23 esv)

Typically the city gates were where community's administrative business was handled. For her husband to sit there meant that he was an influential man, a man known or respected by other leaders. He is respected in part because her daily actions reflected well on the family's reputation.

The Fruit of Her Hands

Finally, we reach the closing verses of this epilogue. They focus the reader specifically on the character she has cultivated and the fruit of her productivity and industry.

> Strength and dignity are her clothing, and she laughs at the time to come. She opens her mouth with wisdom, and the teaching of kindness is on her tongue. She looks well to the ways of her household and does not eat the bread of idleness. Her children rise up and call her blessed; her husband also, and he praises her: "Many women have done excellently, but you surpass

them all." Charm is deceitful, and beauty is vain, but
a woman who fears the Lord is to be praised. Give her
of the fruit of her hands, and let her works praise her
in the gates. (vv. 25–31 ESV)

Most Christian women have heard plenty of messages about beauty,
but how many have heard it in the context of productivity? She may be
beautiful, but that's not the reason why she gets a shout-out in the city
gates. This virtuous woman is praiseworthy because she has "done excel-
lently." It's her hard work that earns her commendation. Motivated by a
love and respect for the Lord—her crowning virtue—her work is fruitful, praiseworthy, and excellent. The fruit of her diligent labors marks
the final sentence in this Old Testament book of wisdom.

The timeless truths we find in the accounts of Lydia and the
Proverbs 31 woman are applicable to us today. Their stories are an essential part of the larger story of work that has been unfolding through our
exploration of history.

The Theology of Work

We've finished telling you a long story about work. We have told you our experience of work and given you an overview narrative of women at work throughout history.

Now we arrive at the theology of work. In this section, we are not addressing practical questions about work and life outside our jobs. We are asking *why* we work, which reaches deep into the core of our longings and desires.

Most of us want someone to tell us that we are making the right choices. We have real questions about our work, but mostly we want assurance that we are doing the best we can do. This book can't assuage that need, nor is it going to answer every possible question about work. What we are confident of, however, is that Jesus remains a faithful shepherd to His people and that He is still fully capable of providing answers for every question and resources for every need.

So we follow Him. The way is the path of discipleship. Every Christian woman is called to be a disciple of Christ and to "work out your own salvation with fear and trembling" (Phil. 2:12 ESV). How that looks is going to be unique to you, because "it is God who works in you, both to will and to work for his good pleasure" (v. 13). The Bible is not vocationally specific, such as telling all Christians to be lawyers or doctors, but it does tell us that as His redeemed children, we are called to love and follow Him. Why? Because He has a plan of redemption and that is what He is working out. Because we are incapable of providing all the answers, we want to point you to the one answer we do have: trust God to work in you.

This brings us back to the idea of a "flat earth fact." Because there are historical and cultural assumptions that shape our ideas about women and work, we will only be able to discern false ideas masquerading as truth by lining them up against God's design for work. That's why in these upcoming chapters we will look at God's purpose for work, the struggles we have in finding our identity in work, how and why to cease work and rest, and what ambition looks like in a Christ-following woman.

CHAPTER 5

Purpose

Every single book we've read on the topic of women and work spends 90 percent of the book talking about the problems we all agree on: work *is* hard, we don't have enough time to do it all, and that there are a lot of obstacles to doing it well. Those books end with suggestions like, "we should have more government subsidies for quality child care," and "get your husband to do more household chores." But we all know the solutions have to be bigger than that.

Maybe we need a renewed perspective on why we work: The Bible shows us work is actually a *gift* to us; it gives us purpose in our labors.

A Garden to Work

The opening words of the Gospel of John give us a poetic introduction to the work of God at the dawn of time:

> In the beginning was the Word, and the Word was
> with God, and the Word was God. He was with God
> in the beginning. All things were created through
> Him, and apart from Him not one thing was created
> that has been created. (John 1:1–3)

The Word—Jesus—is God. As part of the Trinity, Jesus carried out the Father's spoken decrees to bring the world into existence (Gen. 1), creating light and darkness; land and sea; plants and animals; and the stars, sun, and moon. If you picture Genesis as a movie, when the opening credits start rolling, the very first scene is God at work. But you can't see anything because the screen is black. Then, out of the darkness, God's

voice can be heard: "Let there be light." *Flash*—there's light. God begins
His work of creation.

With every new addition to creation, the Father pronounces it good.
Then He makes something He pronounces *very* good:

> Then God said, "Let Us make man in Our image,
> according to Our likeness. They will rule the fish
> of the sea, the birds of the sky, the livestock, all the
> earth, and the creatures that crawl on the earth."
> So God created man in His own image; He created
> him in the image of God; He created them male and
> female. God blessed them, and God said to them, "Be
> fruitful, multiply, fill the earth, and subdue it. Rule
> the fish of the sea, the birds of the sky, and every crea-
> ture that crawls on the earth." (Gen. 1:26–28)

Wait. Hit the pause button because this is the good stuff. In the
very first action word that follows the creation of mankind, we find our
purpose: to fill and subdue the world. Not like some monarch who issues
impossible demands so that all her servants scurry to accomplish her
will. We are created to subdue, or rule over, the world so that our labors
imitate our working, creative God. Verse 28 expands clearly upon that
concept with this command—given to *both* male and female—"be fruitful, multiply, fill the earth, and subdue it." In the paradise God created,
human beings were designed to work and it was called *very* good. Work
is how we imitate God. "When God created people and placed them in
a perfect garden, work was part of his provision to give life meaning,"
theologian Leland Ryken writes. "It can still have that purpose today."[1]

Genesis 2 amplifies the creation account. To continue our movie
analogy, this is where the lighting gets softer and the music changes to
something promising with a hint of romance. Things are about to get
good. In Genesis 2:15, we see that "the LORD God took the man and
placed him in the garden of Eden to work it and watch over it." After
giving Adam a purpose, God then gives him companionship: "Then the
LORD God said, 'It is not good for the man to be alone. I will make a
helper as his complement'" (v. 18).

God knew Adam could not do his job alone. He needed a "helper
suitable" or a "complement" to him. This Hebrew word used in Genesis

2:18 for helper, *'ezer*, is a name by which God is also called in the Old Testament, as one who helps His people. This calling as a "helper" is a way women uniquely bear God's image in our relationships and in our labors. For married women, it is a specific role to be a complement to your husband, but there is a sense in which all women are called to imitate God as a helper. Even when we are in positions of management or leadership at work, being a helper is not a contradictory idea because it is an aspect of God's nature. Jesus showed us what helping looked like as He served His disciples, even though He was a leader. (There is more to this idea and how we can apply it, which we will develop further in the "coaching for success" chapter.)

Adam obviously delighted in Eve and therefore he gave her a name that means *life-giver* or *mother*, which expressed his joy to have her help in doing this work. Adam received Eve as a companion, not as a creature subservient to him. In their partnership, we see that work is a shared calling.

A Garden to Leave

All of this love and joyful productivity—what a sight to behold! But now something slithers across paradise, poised to ruin the harmony. Enter the crafty serpent. Boldly he challenged God's authority with a simple question to Eve: "Did God really say, 'You can't eat from any tree in the garden'?" Eve fell for the serpent's twisted logic, Adam didn't intervene, and both of them defied God by eating the forbidden fruit from the tree in the middle of the garden. Sin—which is rebellion against God's loving authority—was now on the scene and God had a few words about the implications:

> He said to the woman: I will intensify your labor
> pains; you will bear children in anguish. Your desire
> will be for your husband, yet he will rule over you.
> And He said to Adam, "Because you listened to
> your wife's voice and ate from the tree about which
> I commanded you, 'Do not eat from it': The ground
> is cursed because of you. You will eat from it by
> means of painful labor all the days of your life. It will

produce thorns and thistles for you, and you will eat
the plants of the field. You will eat bread by the sweat
of your brow until you return to the ground, since
you were taken from it. For you are dust, and you will
return to dust." (Gen. 3:16–19)

The serpent had lied when he told Eve she would not die (v. 4).
Adam and Eve would soon taste death. Their loving union with God
and between themselves was forever altered, and the joyful productivity
they once enjoyed was already decaying.

The curse meant that Adam and Eve and all who would follow
would now have to work in pain and toil, whether that's laboring in
childbirth or laboring for daily bread. Because of the Fall, in our work
we can have moments of joy as image-bearers of the God who works and
moments of pain and frustration because of the Fall. The good purpose
of productivity remains, but now it's work that must be done among the
thorns and thistles.

Sin is what makes work difficult. As W. R. Forrester says, "man was
meant to be a gardener, but by reason of his sin he became a farmer."[2]

Rule and Subdue

Subduing thorns and thistles is hard work. The concept of work
that emerges from Scripture implies intensity, raw energy, and a pioneer-
ing spirit. When God called men and women to work, he didn't intend
for women to sit on the sidelines watching the men sweat. Women are
to feel the weight of the work we're called to do.

The original command to be productive did not change with the
Fall, it only got harder. These words—be fruitful, multiply, fill the earth,
subdue, and rule (have dominion)—reflect not only God's intentions for
procreation but also a calling to bring a yield from the earth through our
work. The *ESV Study Bible* helps us to understand the original Hebrew:

> The term "subdue" (Hb. *kabash*) elsewhere means to
> bring a people or a land into subjection so that it will
> yield service to the one subduing it (Num. 32:22,
> 29). Here the idea is that the man and woman are to
> make the earth's resources beneficial for themselves,

which implies that they would investigate and
develop the earth's resources to make them useful
for human beings generally. This command provides
a foundation for wise scientific and technological
development.[3]

This call is not negotiable. Women as well as men are called to work. The fourth commandment says, "Six days you shall work, but on the seventh day you shall rest" (Exod. 34:21 ESV). If we believe the authority of Scripture, we must walk in obedience and work, rejecting any and all passivity toward work.

Transformed Work

Fortunately, the corruption of work found in Genesis 3 is not the final word on work. The New Testament brings us much hope that the gospel can transform everything, even our work.

Mark 6:3 tells us that Jesus was a craftsman, the son of a craftsman. The Greek word used there is *tekton*, which means one who works with his hands. Jesus could have worked with wood, stone, or metal—the word is not specific to the material, but rather to the task of building. Jesus worked quietly for most of His adult life as a craftsman. He would have wiped the sweat from His forehead as He worked with raw manpower and bare hands. With every swing of His arm, Jesus experienced the curse of work in a fallen world. But because He came to reverse the curse on this fallen world, the triumph of Jesus' death and resurrection means He has redeemed our futile labors too. He became the curse for us (Gal. 3:13). We are now set free to live (and work) for Jesus.

God knows we are incapable of achieving the perfection that Adam and Eve knew in the garden before sin, and that we still wait for the glorification of heaven, so He provides hope and help for right now. If we believe in Christ as our Savior, He gives us the hope of glory. "We have also obtained access through Him by faith into this grace in which we stand, and we rejoice in the hope of the glory of God" (Rom. 5:2). He gives us the future hope that one day our struggle against sin will be over and our work will be rewarded (Heb. 10:35–39).

He also gives us the grace we need to *transform* our daily work
right now. Most days, this is what we need to remember. How does He
do this? God transforms our work by first transforming us. This is the
effect of the gospel on our work: God gives us hope that He can take our
less-than-perfect attitude about work and sanctify it, all because we are
united with Christ. He takes what we have (which isn't much) into His
perfection, giving it all the qualities we don't possess.

Knowing this helps us to avoid segregating work into secular and
sacred categories—for to God, all work is a sacred calling. This idea is
underscored by how the word in Genesis 2:15 used for work, *'ābad*, is
also used to describe the sacrificial worship that priests performed at the
tabernacle and temple.[4] Work and worship are comingled in the Bible
and can be a reality for our lives.

The leaders of the Reformation fought hard to bring that dignity
back to work, so that no matter what we are doing, we can see it as work
done for God. This is one of the central doctrines of the Reformation.
As Martin Luther wrote, "The works of monks and priests, however holy
and arduous they be, do not differ one whit in the sight of God from
the works of the rustic laborer in the field or the woman going about
her household tasks, but that all works are measured before God by faith
alone."[5] Ryken adds:

> The Reformers began by rejecting the medieval divi-
> sion of work into sacred and secular. To this rejection
> they added the doctrine of vocation or calling, by
> which they meant that God calls people to tasks in
> the world. Thus all work done for God's glory was
> sacred. . . . The cornerstone of Protestant thought
> was the sovereignty of God over all of life, and from
> this flowed an awareness of God's creation of the
> world and his providential concern for it. Given this
> affirmation of the world in which God has placed his
> creatures as stewards, it was inevitable that the Refor-
> mation tradition attached dignity to human work in
> the world.[6]

A Co-Labor of Love

Martin Luther's great contribution to the Reformation—the doctrine of vocation—gives us a word picture to help us think about what transformed work looks like. It is a co-labor of love. Luther interpreted Christ's command against being anxious for food, drink, or clothing (Matt. 6:25) as evidence that God works through our labors: "He gives the wool, but not without our labor. If it is on the sheep, it makes no garment."[7] God gives the wool, but it must be sheared, combed, spun, and made into a garment before His promise is fulfilled. To Luther, our jobs are workshops on how to love our neighbors:

> If you are a craftsman you will find the Bible placed
> in your workshop, in your hands, in your heart; it
> teaches and preaches how you ought to treat your
> neighbor. Only look at your tools, your needle, your
> thimble, your beer barrel, your articles of trade, your
> scales, your measures, and you will find this saying
> written on them. You will not be able to look any-
> where where it does not strike your eyes. None of the
> things with which you deal daily are too trifling to
> tell you this incessantly, if you are but willing to hear
> it; and there is no lack of such preaching, for you have
> as many preachers as there are transactions, com-
> modities, tools, and other implements in your house
> and estate; and they shout this to your face, ". . . use
> me toward your neighbor as you would want him to
> act toward you with that which is his."[8]

In the biblical narrative, our work is a co-labor of love with our Creator *for the benefit of others*. Is someone hungry? Jesus tells her to pray for daily bread. So she asks the heavenly Father to give her the good gift of food. In the way God has ordered this world, His image-bearers co-labor with Him to grow the grain, harvest it, bake the bread, deliver it to the stores, and sell it to hungry people. She receives her daily bread because dozens upon dozens of others were faithful in their labors. Their work embodied answered prayers.

Our daily labors—be they in the marketplace or home—are opportunities for us to love others through our efforts. What we are called to do is not as important as *how* we do it. Because our Creator is working through us to accomplish His redemptive agenda, He transforms our labors among the thistles and the thorns to transactions of love.

Purpose Redefined

We know that work is hard and it can be tempting to ask yourself the reason for why you work. When it feels meaningless—when you are cleaning up behind your toddlers for the umpteenth time in the same day or when you find yourself in yet another boring meeting—it's important to remember that God is working through you even in the most mundane tasks. The antidote to this feeling of meaningless is remembering that our Creator has given dignity to our work.

The Bible redefines our purpose for work. It was His idea in the first place and He continues to work: "For it is God who is working in you, enabling you both to desire and to work out His good purpose" (Phil. 2:13).

As Leland Ryken writes, "If God works, work is good and necessary. It is as simple as that. God's work is a model for human work, showing us that human work in the world is worth doing in a purposive, enjoyable, and fulfilling manner."[9]

CHAPTER 6

Rest

As a little kid, nothing made me happier than the news of a snow day. My sisters and I would climb into Mom's bed together and listen for the radio announcement that our school was closed. Then we'd all curl up for a bit and go back to sleep, pleased to have a lazy start to an unexpected day off.

Even as a young adult, I would get excited about snow days. I never had the kind of job that was deemed essential—such as doctors, nurses, or paramedics—so I would make sure to stock up with rented movies if snow was in the forecast.

Snow days force us to stop and rest. It's a free pass to ignore piled up tasks and unmet deadlines simply because of the weather. But we don't have to wait until winter to enjoy days of rest. Rest is part of the rhythm of work that God designed for us.

Unfortunately, most of us ignore that benefit and make ourselves miserable doing it. We're usually operating at breakneck speed, going from task to task, event to event, from morning to night. The cell phone is buzzing, the microwave is beeping, and our engines are roaring down the road. The frenetic pace of our lives, whether we're shuttling children back and forth to schools and sports or facing the looming projects at work, drives us to neglect the need for rest. We live tired. We think we can overcome it if we take more vitamins, get back to exercising, or drink more coffee. The problem is that we aren't looking to rest. There's too much to do.

But we don't have to live that way. Just as the Genesis account of creation shows us that God worked, it also shows us that God rested.

> Thus the heavens and the earth were finished, and
> all the host of them. And on the seventh day God
> finished his work that he had done, and he rested on
> the seventh day from all his work that he had done.
> So God blessed the seventh day and made it holy,
> because on it God rested from all his work that he had
> done in creation. (Gen. 2:1–3 ESV)

It's not like the eternal and omnipotent God *needed* to rest from His labors. But there it is, right in the creation account. After speaking all of creation into being, God ceased work. In doing so, He modeled for us a rhythm of labor and rest.

Death from Overwork

In Japan, there is a term for the overworked employee who dies early due to job-related stress: *karoshi*. It literally means "death from overwork." Japan's spectacular rise from the ashes of World War II to economic prominence was on the backs of employees who worked for twelve or more hours a day, six or seven days a week, without vacations. The nation achieved great economic progress, but it came at a stiff price: some studies have linked it to increased heart and brain diseases and the decreased life expectancy for Japanese men.

The writer of Ecclesiastes knew the futility of such pursuits. Ecclesiastes 4:6 says: "Better one handful with rest than two handfuls with effort and a pursuit of the wind." Working without rest is both physical and spiritual *karoshi*. Whatever we are chasing in our unceasing labors—fame, fortune, approval—will blow right through our fingers, like pursuing the wind. We can't hold on to it.

Western culture has known for nearly two centuries that a third of our day needs to be for rest, a third of our day for work, and a third of our day for living. As a recent article in *Salon* points out, "150 years of research proves that long hours at work kill profits, productivity and employees . . . every hour you work over 40 hours a week is making you less effective and productive over both the short and the long haul. And it may sound weird, but it's true: the single easiest, fastest thing your company can do to boost its output and profits—starting right now, today—is to get everybody off the 55-hour-a-week treadmill, and back onto a 40-hour footing."[1]

Even if we try to push ourselves, we may not be accomplishing very much. There is only One being who gets everything done on His to-do list. This is the point of Psalm 127, which echoes the themes found in Ecclesiastes:

> Unless the LORD builds a house, its builders labor over
> it in vain; unless the LORD watches over a city, the
> watchman stays alert in vain. In vain you get up early
> and stay up late, working hard to have enough food—
> yes, He gives sleep to the one He loves. (Ps. 127:1–2)

There is an alternate reading for that last line, which is even more encouraging: "yes, He gives such things to His loved ones while [they] sleep."

As a self-employed person, I (Carolyn) have had that experience too many times to count—where I've needed to find new assignments or clients but haven't any lined up. Then I've awakened the next day to find an unsolicited job offer in my e-mail. This isn't restricted to those of us who are self-employed, but I think it's easier to be aware of this daily provision when you don't have any assumptions about the source of your income.

I've also had the opposite experience, where I've pushed myself past my creaturely needs for sleep and thought I was making lots of progress—only to review my work after I've had some sleep and realized how poor it really was. It was vain to stay up that late after all. (*Ouch. That's Nora, poking me in the side because this happened throughout the writing of this book! She's the early bird and I'm the night owl, but many of my late night writing efforts were shown to be incoherent by the light of day. I need the truth of my own chapter and I'm not too proud to say so.*)

If we recognize the essential difference between God and us, we see the foolishness of ignoring God's command to rest. Tim Challies writes:

> Remember your created limits. So much of worka-
> holism is a defiance of the physical limitations that
> God our creator has imposed upon us. Remember

that the Lord has also put a curse on work. Knowing
that fallen man would seek ultimate satisfaction in
his work, rather than in Him, God built in "thorns
and thistles and sweat" to drive man from work to
Himself.[2]

Many wives and mothers are well aware of their creaturely limits,
but see no end in sight for their work. I (Nora) empathize. Rest is elusive
for busy moms. Sleep is sporadic at best and from the stories I hear, teen-
agers encroach on your nights just as much as toddlers. Reading that last
line from Psalm 127—"He gives sleep to the one He loves"—you could
be thinking, "By the few hours of sleep I get, God must not love me that
much." But here's real encouragement for you: God provides us rest in
our spirit through the grace He provides. Even in our creaturely need
for rest, God draws us to Himself to sustain us in supernatural ways.

Rest is not mere inactivity. It's also restorative. There are elements
of rest that are mentally and spiritually restorative, as well. The military often refers to time off as "R&R," meaning "rest and recreation."
Recreation—doing something other than what we do as our vocation—
can be very restful for the mind. Years ago, I (Carolyn) heard a sermon
series about rest, and the message about recreation as part of rest really
sunk in with me. At the time, I lived less than ten minutes away from a
large lake where I could kayak. An hour spent on the water on Sunday
afternoons was more rejuvenating than an extra hour of sleep. It felt like
a mini-vacation. Being outside, enjoying the beauty of the water was a
stark contrast to my computer-based labor at an office.

Rest is meant to restore our capacity for work. If we work without
resting, we are shutting down the creative parts of ourselves, causing
all of our mental capabilities to retreat deep into the part of our brain
wired for survival. Sleep is important, but so are other restorative activities like exercise, nourishing food, time with friends, or reading a good
book. Following God's pattern of weekly rest may be the best part of
productivity.

Although we are made to be in the image of God, we are not like
God in His limitless abilities—only He does not slumber or sleep (Ps.
121:4). Therefore, in this chapter we will look at three aspects of rest: the
resources to rest, the mark of rest, and the gift of rest.

Resources to Rest

When we think of people living in biblical times, we can picture the static nativity scene, where everyone is in a frozen tableau of perpetual rest. But that's not reality, certainly not for the Israelites when they were enslaved in Egypt. They were afflicted with unceasing work making bricks—and without the straw they needed to make them. So they cried out to the Lord for relief and He heard them (Exod. 2:23–25). Through Moses, the Lord delivered them from slavery and sent them on a journey to "a good and spacious land, a land flowing with milk and honey" (Exod. 3:8).

But the journey was long and arduous, so the Israelites quickly forgot God's promised future and the misery of their past. They grumbled about being hungry in the desert, wistfully recalling "when we sat by pots of meat and ate all the bread we wanted" (Exod. 16:3). Worse, they charged Moses with negligent leadership, saying "you brought us into this wilderness to make this whole assembly die of hunger!"

The Lord heard their complaints and decided to "rain bread from heaven" for them. For six days, manna would show up on the desert surface—a flaky substance similar to a sweet wafer. There was always enough for each person to collect two quarts. But on the seventh day, no manna would appear. The double portion of manna that the Israelites collected on the sixth day would stay fresh on the seventh day—unlike the rest of the week—so that the Israelites could cease gathering food and rest. But not everyone believed the provision would come as God promised.

> Yet on the seventh day some of the people went out to gather, but they did not find any. Then the LORD said to Moses, "How long will you refuse to keep My commands and instructions? Understand that the LORD has given you the Sabbath; therefore on the sixth day He will give you two days' worth of bread. Each of you stay where you are; no one is to leave his place on the seventh day." So the people rested on the seventh day. (Exod. 16:27–30)

After initially disobeying these commands, the Israelites learned an important lesson about rest: *God will provide the necessary resources to cease daily labors.* In His kingdom, it's not necessary to work continuously. He can be trusted to provide what we need to take a break—an incredible promise! We serve a God who gives us both a purpose for our labors and resources for our rest.

The Mark of Rest

There's another aspect of rest found in this story. When Moses presented the Ten Commandments, the Israelites learned that God has another purpose for rest: *the Sabbath marks God's people as being set apart for His glory.*

> The LORD said to Moses: "Tell the Israelites: You must
> observe My Sabbaths, for it is a sign between Me and
> you throughout your generations, so that you will
> know that I am Yahweh who sets you apart. Observe
> the Sabbath, for it is holy to you." (Exod. 31:12–14)

In stark contrast to the surrounding cultures, where work never ceased, the Lord gave His people a day to rest. Then He told them why: a day of rest, the Sabbath, was a sign of the covenant between them and their God. It was an outward expression of their trust in God, a physical demonstration of worship to those looking on. Resting set them apart from the way the rest of the world operated.

This is the point of God's rebuke in Isaiah 30. He tells His people that they have put their confidence in an alliance with Egypt without consulting Him (*Egypt*—where they used to be slaves!) and have not rested in His promises to take care of them. They traded rest and provision for oppression and deceit.

> This is what the Sovereign LORD, the Holy One of
> Israel, says: "In repentance and rest is your salvation,
> in quietness and trust is your strength, but you would
> have none of it. You said, 'No, we will flee on horses.'
> Therefore you will flee! You said, 'We will ride off on
> swift horses.'" (Isa. 30:15–16 NIV)

For years, I had this verse on some artwork that hung near the spot where I had my devotions. It was a visible reminder that my strength is not found in myself but in my God whom I trust. Resting is a choice of faith—a physical act of saying God will keep His promises. This is not a modern problem. While technology may have amped up the distractions, quietness and trust before the Lord is an age-old issue. We may not think swift horses will save us, but our work patterns reveal what we *do* think will save us.

More importantly, the mark of rest shows that we are liberated people. Tim Keller elaborates:

> God liberated his people when they were slaves in Egypt, and in Deuteronomy 5:12–15, God ties the Sabbath to freedom from slavery. Anyone who overworks is really a slave. Anyone who cannot rest from work is a slave—to a need for success, to a materialistic culture, to exploitative employers, to parental expectations, or to all of the above. These slave masters will abuse you if you are not disciplined in the practice of Sabbath rest. Sabbath is a declaration of freedom.
>
> Thus Sabbath is about more than external rest of the body; it is about inner rest of the soul. We need rest from the anxiety and strain of our overwork, which is really an attempt to justify ourselves—to gain the money or the status or the reputation we think we have to have. Avoiding overwork requires deep rest in Christ's finished work for your salvation (Hebrews 4:1–10). Only then will you be able to "walk away" regularly from your vocational work and rest.[3]

Walking away from vocation work can be hard in certain periods of your life. It would be hypocritical of me if I extolled the virtues of Sabbath rest without confessing that I didn't have much rest while writing this book—at least not as the deadline loomed large over my life. At first I felt condemned by my own words as I wrote this chapter. But then I found myself rejoicing in a God who allows—even commands—a way out from this crushing burden of work! So for those who are feeling the same way, here is further advice from Tim Keller about the seasons and cycles of rest:

> Israel's Sabbath cycles of rest-and-work included not only Sabbath days but also Sabbath years and even a Year of Jubilee every forty-nine years (Lev. 25:8–11). This is a crucial insight for workers in today's world. It is possible to voluntarily take on a season of work that requires high energy, long hours, and insufficient weekly-Sabbath time. A new physician has to work long hours in a residency program, for example, and many other careers (such as finance, government, and law) similarly demand some sort of initial period of heavy, intense work. Starting your own business or pursuing a major project like making a movie will require something similar. In these situations you have to watch that you don't justify too little Sabbath by saying you're "going through a season"—when in actual fact that season never ends.
>
> If you must enter a season like this, it should not last longer than two or three years at the most. Be accountable to someone for this, or you will get locked into an "under-Sabbathed" lifestyle, and you will burn out. And during this "under-Sabbathed" time, do not let the rhythms of prayer, Bible study, and worship die. Be creative, but get it in.[4]

The Gift of Rest

As we've seen so far, rest teaches us to trust God to provide for us and it makes us stop and worship the God who gives us rest. These concepts also point to the most obvious and important aspect of rest: *it is a gift to us,* a gift that is foreshadowed in the Old Testament and wholly fulfilled by the New Testament in three very important words uttered at the cross: "It is finished."

The curse that all human beings have lived under since Adam and Eve were expelled from the garden of Eden was reversed by the atoning work of Jesus as He hung on the cross and died for our sins. The most important work we could ever aspire to do would be to earn our way back into God's favor. But this is utterly impossible for "all have sinned and fall short of the glory of God" (Rom. 3:23). There is no way we could ever work hard enough to be readmitted to paradise.

But Jesus did! His work was perfectly acceptable to the Father and He freely shares it with those who would believe Him to be sufficient. Rest in this age and in the age to come are gifts from a merciful God who does not overlook justice but righteously poured out His wrath on His perfect Son who became our substitute to take the punishment we deserved. If we think anything else will be acceptable to the Father, we are sorely mistaken.

This is what Jesus was demonstrating to us when He performed good works on the Sabbath. He healed the man with the withered hand, the woman who was unable to stand straight, the man with dropsy, the paralytic at the Pool of Bethesda, and the man born blind on the Sabbath. In doing so, He was making a point to those who stood there judging Him for it: *human obedience does not make the Sabbath.* Jesus is the Lord of the Sabbath and He *gives* it to His people, just as He gives the ultimate rest in being justified from our sins.

> "Come to Me, all of you who are weary and bur-
> dened, and I will give you rest. All of you, take up
> My yoke and learn from Me, because I am gentle and
> humble in heart, and you will find rest for yourselves.
> For My yoke is easy and My burden is light." (Matt.
> 11:28–30)

Jesus beckons to us, promising the rest we need for all eternity. In taking on His "yoke," we will learn from Him, walking in His provision for work and rest in this life, and rejoicing in His humility that made Him willing to take our place at the cross so we could enter into His rest for all eternity.

Thanks be to our Lord and Savior, "it is finished"!

CHAPTER 7

Identity

Several years ago, I spoke to a friend at a church event who had been influential as a lawyer for the cause and practice of religious freedom. She had been single for many years, but was now recently married and a first-time mother. As we caught up with each other, she confessed that her transition from being a lawyer to being a stay-at-home mother with an infant was a lot harder than she anticipated.

"As much as I love being married and a mom, after all these years being single, I just didn't realize how much I drew upon my work as the source of my identity," she said with a small smile.

It's very easy to confuse *what we do* with *who we are*. As one sociologist said, "Most people define themselves by their job. When they retire, they need a narrative about who they are now."[1]

There are many narratives we have developed for and about ourselves. In my office, we jokingly refer to this as a tap-dancing moment. That's because one of my coworkers said she grew up thinking she was really good at tap dancing. There wasn't much else she excelled at in her childhood, but she could always fall back on her tap-dancing skills to be assured of her self-worth. Then one day as an adult, she pulled out her dance videos to show them to her friends. As she watched, she had a sudden shift in perspective. Her cherished narrative about being a good tap dancer was being challenged by the evidence before her.

"I was shocked to see how I wasn't very good after all," she said, laughing. "All these years, I thought I was a fairly decent tap dancer but my self-deception crumbled with the evidence on tape!"

Though we can encounter the things that trigger a crisis of identity almost anywhere, one of the most painful places to encounter them is in church. Single women can feel competent all week at work and then feel like awkward third wheels in churches bursting with young families. Young mothers can remember when they knew what was going on in culture and world news, but now they hover seemingly invisible near laughing young single adults who talk about the latest bands, restaurants, and entertainment. Older mothers feel empty when their teens are more interested in their peers than in their families. Widows grieve for their identities as wives and mourn the loss of their social lives as part of a couple. As the church caters to different stages of life, we can feel more like walking demographic labels than women of diverse life experiences.

Any change in what we do can easily trigger a crisis of identity— what is the story we are now to tell others about ourselves? While I think this is true for men, I think it is different, and perhaps more pronounced, for women because our productivity choices are scrutinized more often than those of men.

That's why the most divisive terms may be the dreaded "working mothers" versus "stay-at-home mothers." If it were a simple description of the location of female productivity, that would be one thing. But these phrases are loaded with guilt and judgment. That's why I appreciated the letter I received from a friend of mine as I worked on this book. I've thought about it a lot because it hits not only upon the issue of identity, but also how we can judge the choices of others:

> I have been a working mom for a couple of years now. Not something I *ever* saw myself doing. I've gone from a homeschooling mom of seven children to a grandmother of eleven who is out working for the first time in decades!
>
> While God has been kind to protect me from self-righteousness and superiority in relation to working mothers (having a hard-working single mom for a sister helped!), I've experienced gracious conviction over the past couple of years as God has allowed me to get to know devoted, loving moms who have never homeschooled or stayed at home full-time with their kids, yet LOVE them just a fiercely as I do. I've known that "intellectually," but now I've seen it, observed it up close, and been convicted by my subtly condescending attitudes toward working moms.

As much as change can challenge our own identities, time and experience often shift our perspectives about the identities of others too. But there's a more important perspective shift about identity that Jesus offers us.

At His Feet

I have this crazy photo, a screen grab from the moment when Austrian skydiver Felix Baumgartner looked down at Earth from his capsule 125,000 feet high above our planet. He was only moments away from casually leaning over and falling toward Earth at supersonic speeds. My stomach churned with the queasy thought of being that high, yet I couldn't tear my eyes away from the live feed. I was transfixed by the perspective he had. All of our striving, conflict, greed, and sin seemed peacefully erased from his view. Yet he was about to hurl himself right back into it.

You don't have to be a daredevil to change your perspective. Jesus once offered two women an escape from their earthbound viewpoints too. Yes, you know it—I'm going to drag out our poster girls, Mary and Martha. But I won't tell you to be more contemplative/laid-back/devoted or less busy/administrative/cranky (okay, maybe less cranky). Nor will I offer you any time-management tips from these sisters. I just want you to consider the perspective shift Jesus handed them all that day—men and women alike.

In Luke's account, Jesus had just blown up the issue of identity with the story of the Good Samaritan. A lawyer had challenged Him about the neighbor he must love as himself (Luke 10:29), and Jesus gave him a merciful Samaritan, a despised ethnic group living nearby. Then "as they went on their way" Jesus led them to the home of Martha and Mary. Martha immediately went into high gear with the work of hosting Jesus and His disciples. But Mary sat at His feet with the men, listening to Jesus instructing His disciples. Unlike most rabbis of His time, Jesus not only allowed a woman to learn the Scriptures, He also told everyone present that this was the wisest thing Mary could do—"Mary has chosen the good portion, which will not be taken away from her" (v. 42 ESV).

No husbands were mentioned for either of these women. No children were mentioned, either. Perhaps they had them once. Perhaps they would have them in the future. No mention was made of their social status, either by wealth or social connections or job skills. But their one identity that was most important was the one that would exist forever: a follower of Christ.

This is the identity we need to affirm among ourselves, not the labels that come with the kind of labor we do. As Christians, we are to be grounded in this identity, even as we add other roles and ways to express that identity in relationship to others. We might have an interesting job for a season. We might be married for a season. We might have children at home for a season. *But those things can be taken away from us or never given to us at all. They are gifts for this life only.*

Jesus has promised that if we choose to sit at His feet, we have made the best choice of all. We will inherit the better portion, that which will never be taken away: a relationship with God, His Word, and the promise of eternal rewards and life with Him in heaven. In one simple sentence, Jesus shifts our earthbound perspective and takes us high above our daily lives to see the importance of being His disciple.

The Awl in My Ear

From the outside looking in, being a filmmaker can appear to be a glamorous profession. But most people have no idea how many hours my backside is glued to a chair, editing scripts, transcribing interviews, paying bills, and writing bleary e-mails after midnight. It appears to be glamorous because our culture applauds creative professions. But if you could watch the daily time-lapse of my office activities, you'd be bored into a stupor.

Even though a lot of people respond enthusiastically to what I do professionally, if I say I'm a Christian, only some people light up in response. Others try to shuffle away, avoiding further eye contact with me in case I try to convert them on the spot.

I can only imagine the responses I would get if I went further and used one of the descriptions God has for me in the Scriptures: I was once a slave to sin and now I'm a slave to Christ, a term the epistle writers often used to open their letters (Rom. 1:1; 2 Tim. 2:24; Titus 1:1; James

1:1; 2 Pet. 1:1). Slavery is an awful term—and for good reason, I might add. It is a terrible aspect of our political history and a current scourge in many nations around the world. Yet the Bible's view of slavery is not quite the same as our modern understanding of forced labor. The Bible speaks of slavery in terms of ownership: Who or what owns you? What has mastered you?

In the Old Testament, there's a crazy commandment regarding slaves that you can find in both Deuteronomy 15 and Exodus 21. It reads:

> If your fellow Hebrew, a man or woman, is sold to
> you and serves you six years, you must set him free
> in the seventh year. When you set him free, do not
> send him away empty-handed. Give generously to
> him from your flock, your threshing floor, and your
> winepress. You are to give him whatever the LORD
> your God has blessed you with. Remember that you
> were a slave in the land of Egypt and the LORD your
> God redeemed you; that is why I am giving you this
> command today. But if your slave says to you, "I
> don't want to leave you," because he loves you and
> your family, and is well off with you, take an awl
> and pierce through his ear into the door, and he will
> become your slave for life. Also treat your female
> slave the same way. Do not regard it as a hardship
> when you set him free, because he worked for you six
> years—worth twice the wages of a hired hand. Then
> the LORD your God will bless you in everything you
> do. (Deut. 15:12–18)

The idea here is that when another Hebrew had fallen onto hard times financially, his or her only remaining asset was the ability to work. Therefore he or she could be sold into slavery to another Hebrew, but only for a specific period of time—unless they wanted to remain a slave. Though this provision exists for someone who is treated well to *choose* to remain in permanent servitude, I know of no record in the Bible or other historical literature where someone actually did so.

So why would the Holy Spirit inspire such a command? It points us to Jesus. In Philippians 2:7–8, it says Jesus "emptied Himself by assuming the form of a slave. And when He had come as a man in His external form, He humbled Himself by becoming obedient to the point of death—even to death on a cross." Jesus chose the position of a slave so as to rescue all of us who are enslaved to our own sins and passions and give us a new identity as one of His slaves. But even though being a slave of Christ is more than we deserve, His bounty does not stop there. Ephesians tells us of an even greater identity as adopted children: "In love He predestined us to be adopted through Jesus Christ for Himself, according to His favor and will, to the praise of His glorious grace that He favored us with in the Beloved" (Eph. 1:4–6).

Better than a benevolent Master, we have a loving Father who has adopted us and made us coheirs with Christ. Our new identities range from slave to heir, and encompass every relational benefit in between.

The awl in my ear, then, is a priceless jewel, beyond compare. It marks me as His, and pales to whatever other identification I might be wearing. Today we might be working hard as homemakers or doctors and loving and serving others as mothers or sisters, but the roles we assume in relationship to other people are not our ultimate identities. You or I might be the boss today, but that will change one day in the future. What doesn't change is the identity Christ has given to us through His divine plan of rescue.

That is the better portion and it will never be taken away from us.

Investing for the Eternal

I have a friend who is an artist. I have several of Heather's paintings in my home—works I commissioned because I wanted to own one of her originals. But Heather often struggles with her identity as an artist. Her circle of art major friends have all gone on to do impressive and cool things in the art world—except for her and one other friend, also a young mother who is busy with her family. Heather is sometimes discouraged by this, even though her husband encourages her to paint in her home studio and ensures she schedules that time. Heather is also an art teacher who is busy inspiring the next generation to love creativity.

But somehow that doesn't feel important enough when she thinks about what her college friends have accomplished.

I hear this from a lot of artists. The Artist identity seems to trump most other identities. But wait. I hear this from my medical friends too. The Surgeon identity seems to trump other labels. Oh, and there's the Designer—graphic, industrial, fashion, or interior—and that identity is pretty all-consuming too. Let's not forget the Chef. Or the Washington, D.C., specialty, where the highest-ranking person is referred to by the position, as in the Senator, the Member, the Chairman. You know you've arrived when you have a large staff and circle of rotating interns who simply refer to you as the Position.

When your work is your identity, change can shake that sense of identity. Comparison to others can drive you to maximize your identity. We all feel it; it is a longing for significance, to be known and recognized, to be validated for our labors and achievements. This is nothing new. Even the author of Ecclesiastes saw this:

> Then I saw that all toil and all skill in work come
> from a man's envy of his neighbor. This also is vanity
> and a striving after wind. (Eccl. 4:4 ESV)

The New Testament version of that insight comes from 1 Timothy 6:6–7 (ESV):

> Now there is great gain in godliness with content-
> ment, for we brought nothing into the world, and we
> cannot take anything out of the world.

Our pastor says that Ecclesiastes challenges the quest for success. You can't justify your existence by what you *do*. You can't justify it through a promotion, a huge bonus, or the ability to feed your family all organic food. You can't justify your existence through your holiday cards or your well-attended speech. You can't justify it through your huge Twitter following or your mommy blog. These attempts to attain some measure of success are vanity, according to Ecclesiastes.

What we long for is perfection—in our works and in who we are. This is only possible through Jesus—Jesus lived the perfect life we can't, paid the penalty for our sins that we can't, and rose from the dead so that one day we will rise if we trust Him for the gift of eternal life. What *needs* to be done has already been done!

Until then, we invest. We invest what we've received so that we multiply His gifts for His glory. Taking on an investor mind-set means that we can let go of our worry about what we have and who we are right now and instead live for the things that are eternal. Not the day we make Employee of the Month. Not the Mother's Day when we're finally holding a baby. Not the day we float down the aisle toward a beaming new husband. Not the day we make partner. Not the day we can finally retire in comfort. Jesus says the day we should live for is when we hear, "Well done, good and faithful servant."

> "For it [the kingdom of heaven] will be like a man going on a journey, who called his servants and entrusted to them his property. To one he gave five talents, to another two, to another one, to each according to his ability. Then he went away. He who had received the five talents went at once and traded with them, and he made five talents more. So also he who had the two talents made two talents more. But he who had received the one talent went and dug in the ground and hid his master's money. Now after a long time the master of those servants came and settled accounts with them. And he who had received the five talents came forward, bringing five talents more, saying, 'Master, you delivered to me five talents; here I have made five talents more.' His master said to him, 'Well done, good and faithful servant. You have been faithful over a little; I will set you over much. Enter into the joy of your master.' And he also who had the two talents came forward, saying, 'Master, you delivered to me two talents; here I have made two talents more.' His master said to him, 'Well done, good and faithful servant. You have been faithful over a little; I will set you over much. Enter into the joy of your master.' He also who had received the one talent came forward, saying, 'Master, I knew you to be a hard man, reaping where you did not sow, and

gathering where you scattered no seed, so I was afraid, and I went and hid your talent in the ground. Here you have what is yours.' But his master answered him, 'You wicked and slothful servant! You knew that I reap where I have not sown and gather where I scattered no seed? Then you ought to have invested my money with the bankers, and at my coming I should have received what was my own with interest. So take the talent from him and give it to him who has the ten talents. For to everyone who has will more be given, and he will have an abundance. But from the one who has not, even what he has will be taken away. And cast the worthless servant into the outer darkness. In that place there will be weeping and gnashing of teeth.'" (Matt. 25:14–30 ESV)

Don't be misled by the small numbers. One talent was about twenty years' worth of wages. It was like winning the lottery even to get *one* talent, so the servant who judged his master's motives and character harshly was truly ungrateful and envious.

An additional point to consider is that twenty years isn't a time frame that lends itself to short-term gain. This passage points us to the importance of stewardship. Just as a retirement account is meant to grow by compounding on the interest earned, Jesus is reminding us that we need to be faithfully investing what He has given us for the long-term gains over our lifetimes.

Stewardship will look very differently for women, but generally, women's lives are broken into twenty-year cycles too. We grow into maturity for the first twenty years; most of us marry and bear children in the next twenty years; we steward our successes and broaden our influence in the community or workplace during the "open nest" years from forty to sixty (a phrase I like much better than "empty nest"), and then we focus on enriching our legacy for the remaining twenty years—concepts we will explore in the last section of the book. While this life arc doesn't work out exactly this way for every woman—myself included—we generally experience something close to this pattern. These twenty-year cycles often introduce new shifts in our identities, but they also present new opportunities for eternal investment.

Expected Volatility

Let's go back to my friend, Heather, for a moment. From my perspective, she has at least two talents in her possession: her art and her family. According to this parable, she will give an account for both. So does that mean she should give both equal attention at all times? I don't think so.

Even in financial terms, a well-balanced portfolio has a mix of asset classes—investments in long-term holdings, aggressive short-term stocks, stable income-paying products, and so forth. The mix should change according to your time line. The goal is to own assets that are uncorrelated, meaning that they don't move in the same direction or the same degree at the same time. This is done so that your investments are diversified. Financial advisors also say that, in any portfolio used for retirement saving, you should know two numbers: expected return and expected volatility. They both affect the performance of the investments.

"Expected volatility"—that's the reason many women scale down their work commitments when they have children. They know children introduce volatility! So perhaps for a season in Heather's life, her art goes into a different asset class, to become more prominent in the future. God willing, Heather will be just as creative, if not more so, later in life. Does that mean she has thrown in the towel on art? Absolutely not. There's the principle of "expected return" to consider—whatever is considered to have the higher return gets more of the investment.

The emphasis Scripture has on the importance of mothering is clear. Being artistically creative to the glory of God is important. But being a mother to the glory of God is paramount. It is important even for those of us who have not had children. Our investments in the next generation through the children who have been given to us as nieces, nephews, or neighbors are just as important. Our work may not be known in ten years, but the children in whom we invested will be (Lord willing). The "expected return" for investing in children is almost invaluable—too precious to measure.

But the shifts between those twenty-year epochs can be bumpy. I have friends who have struggled with the transition to motherhood, and friends who have struggled with the transition out of motherhood. (Though as one friend reminds me, mothering doesn't end once the

children move out from your own home. It just takes on different contours as your children become adults.) That's why locating your identity
in your eternal identity, the "better choice" that will never be taken
away, helps you to shape wise choices for today. Is the "asset" you have
one that needs to be invested in today or can it wait for another season?
Does it need just periodic stirring, so to speak, to maintain your investment, or does it need your full attention right now?

You may recognize that this is essentially the feminist sequencing
discussion that I introduced in chapter 2. To some degree, that's true.
But sequencing, while a practical tool, is not based in the eternal perspective. As we saw earlier, in the Bible the woman most commended
for her productivity was ultimately commended because she feared the
Lord (Prov. 31:30). Sequencing may be a concept that helps you think
about seasons of life, but it can't point you to what's eternally important.

Day of Reckoning

If you ever played the board game of Life, you may remember that
the game ended with the Day of Reckoning where all of your assets were
evaluated—even your spouse and kids were worth money. (I always
loved this game because everyone had to get married. No missing the
honeymoon for me!) The point is, the game always ends. There's no
escaping the Day of Reckoning.

The problem is that we secretly believe the game will never end. We
are surprised when a chapter closes for us—when we realize we'll never
be good enough for professional athletics, or to be the CEO, or to win
an Oscar, or to invent the next hot social media tool. Or perhaps we
have been the CEO or Oscar winner, but now it's time to step into the
shadows and let someone else take over.

If the game of life we're playing is for here and now, we're going to
be shaken. No doubt about it. Remember those last twenty years? The
twilight hours of our lives can be productive if we are still multiplying
what we have for the glory of God. We might not have much money, but
we can give a "widow's mite" with great affection. We might not have an
active career, but we have a lifetime of relationships that still need cultivation and care. We might not be as physically active, but we can bow
our heads in prayer to intercede for people around the world. We might

be "old school," but we have decades of stories about the workings of a faithful God to share with those who are weary in doing good.

Our identities are firmly anchored in Christ. When we manage others, our identity is not the Boss. It's as a slave who knows how sweet it is to labor for Jesus and who tries to emulate the gentleness of our risen Master when we have the privilege of overseeing others. When we make the best-seller list, our identity is not the Hot New Author. We are still the women who sit at Jesus' feet to hear His Word. When we score the winning contract or the final goal, we know the One who gave us those talents to hone via hard work and practice. When our last child moves out, our identity is not the Empty Nester. We're still the same adopted daughter and coheir with Christ that we were while the children were underfoot. In a new season, we have to shift our asset class around and prayerfully discover what else we are to multiply. But our most important part of our identities is unaltered.

We spent the first part of this book talking about the story of work and now we're exploring the theology of work. We still have one more concept—ambition—before we get to the practical issues of work. There's a reason for that: Nora and I cannot tell you how to run your life. We want you to know what's happened in the past and what biblical issues surround and define productivity, but we don't have a bunch of one-size-fits-all rules for you.

Except one: Sit at His feet and not on your buried talents.

CHAPTER 8

Ambition

I have always been ambitious. But often in a crazy, not-totally-grounded-in-reality way.

Exhibit A is the pony episode. When I was around twelve years old, I was desperate to have a pony. Where I was going to put this pony, I don't know. But I pestered my parents daily—until my dad got the bright idea to let me research how I, an unemployed child, could manage the care and feeding of such a large animal. Elated, I ran off to form what would be my very first business plan. I returned with an elaborate proposal to work two jobs (not specified where) to afford the boarding expenses at a broken-down horse farm more than two miles from my home. Apparently I also planned to feed the pony grass clippings from all the lawns I would mow. Not that I had actually mowed any lawns yet—that was a minor detail. Then I would haul the heavy bags of grass clippings by myself those two miles to feed the horse. And, I guess in winter, when there were no lawns to mow, the horse would just go on a diet.

My father, rightly seeing through my shoddy planning, shot me down with a gentle, "Now don't you see why this wouldn't work?" I was inconsolable. How could he deny my desire for a horse?! I wanted a pony *soooooo* badly.

We all want something. That's the drive behind ambition. But in the years since this infamous episode, I've learned this precious truth: we were actually *created* to be this way. God has made us to be people who have desires.

Picture this. A mother approached Jesus. She kneeled to worship Him, but Jesus knew this was a petition.

"What do you want?" He asked her.

"Promise," she said to Him, "that these two sons of mine may sit, one on Your right and the other on Your left, in Your kingdom."

Jesus answered her stage-mother request by addressing her sons. "You don't know what you're asking. Are you able to drink the cup that I am about to drink?"

"We are able," they said to Him, with great confidence.

So Jesus replied: "You will indeed drink My cup. But to sit at My right and left is not Mine to give; instead, it belongs to those for whom it has been prepared by My Father."

At this point, the other men in the group of disciples heard what was going on and they became indignant with the brothers. Such *chutzpah!* But Jesus called them over and gave them a whole new perspective on ambition and prominence:

> "You know that the rulers of the Gentiles dominate
> them, and the men of high position exercise power
> over them. It must not be like that among you. On
> the contrary, whoever wants to become great among
> you must be your servant, and whoever wants to be
> first among you must be your slave; just as the Son of
> Man did not come to be served, but to serve, and to
> give His life—a ransom for many." (Matt. 20:25–28)

Jesus did not chastise anyone in this scene for being ambitious. Instead, He got right to the heart of the matter: *What do you want?* Then He instructed "whoever wants to become great" on exactly how to do it. Which is to say, not quite the way this particular mother did it.

Jesus knows we have desires. This is why He came to Earth. Sin corrupted our drive and our desires. Jesus came to redeem that brokenness and to give us renewed desires.

In another account, while rebuking those who were persecuting Him, Jesus said:

> "I do not accept glory from men, but I know you—
> that you have no love for God within you. I have
> come in My Father's name, yet you don't accept Me.
> If someone else comes in his own name, you will
> accept him. How can you believe? *While accepting*

glory from one another, you don't seek the glory that comes from the only God." (John 5:41–44, emphasis added)

There's no sitting out the glory game. Ambition is just another way to express that effort. We are treasure hunters, ambitiously seeking out what we value. This is why Jesus told us to seek *lasting* treasure: "Don't collect for yourselves treasures on earth, where moth and rust destroy and where thieves break in and steal. But collect for yourselves treasures in heaven, where neither moth nor rust destroys, and where thieves don't break in and steal. For where your treasure is, there your heart will be also" (Matt. 6:19–21). He didn't tell us to quit being ambitious. He just told us to quit being fools amassing useless junk like those poor souls featured on a hoarders program. Go for the gold, Jesus said, the real gold.

The Ambition Gap

When my (Nora's) husband, Travis, would sit up in bed late at night and talk to me about his ambitions, I would snuggle down in the bed and try to listen sincerely. For two years in Arizona, we had been trying to recover from unemployment; more so, we were trying to get off a track that seemed to lead us around in circles. When he would talk about angel investors or futures trading and pester me for startup Internet business ideas, I couldn't understand how he could still aim so high. While Travis was ambitious, I felt very disappointed. I felt like I couldn't be ambitious anymore because we had been disappointed over and over again. The biggest ambition I could muster was for a new piece of furniture.

On my way to work one morning, I called my grandmother. All my woes spilled out with a cascade of tears. She listened quietly, and then she told me one of her stories.

She got married at twenty-five—later in life than most in that post-WWII culture—to my grandfather, a man with mixed ambitions. He was a trained concert pianist, yet he was told to leave those dreams behind and pursue something more practical, so he became an economist instead. He was still ambitious, studying at the Sorbonne in Paris, and writing articles in his field; but in one area he wasn't as ambitious: my grandmother's career. When they married, my grandmother was in night school to become a doctor. He told her that she could continue her studies, if she wanted, but that she had to choose between being a mother or a doctor. Though my grandmother wanted to be a doctor, she chose motherhood and became a certified physician assistant instead.

Talking to her that day, my grandmother reminded me that dreams always come with a cost. She reminded me that I wasn't the first or the last one to wrestle with my ambitions, and the twisted trails of disappointments on which they might take you.

A prominent business leader, Sheryl Sandberg, says there is an "ambition gap" between men and women. She says women have negative feelings about ambition because success and likability are positively correlated to men, but negatively correlated to women: "As a man gets more powerful and successful, he is better liked. As a woman gets more powerful and successful, she is less liked."[1]

Sandberg says we need to "lean in" and yet it's not easy in the face of reality. I wasn't shying away from success and ambition, but I was weary of how hard work can be. As a young woman, I had lots of ambitions and big dreams. What had happened?

So I dug in to do some research. I read more of my husband's books about work and I studied the Bible. I talked to lots of people and I surfed the Internet. That's when I realized it's true—I *did* have an ambition gap. But it was a bigger problem than not having the desire to be a top corporate executive. It was also way bigger than not liking to be known as an ambitious woman.

I discovered I had a major gap between my concept of ambition and what the Bible says about it. Ambition isn't just for men, it isn't just for business—it's an essential component of being human. Sometimes in church circles, we talk more about contentment (which is a good thing) but it can minimize the importance of ambition—that somehow it is more spiritual for Christians to be passive. This misunderstanding had slowed me down to the point where I wasn't moving ahead at all.

I learned that ambition is really a desire to grow. I realized that in order for me to obey God's call to be "fruitful and multiply" (Gen. 1:28), I needed to stop shutting down ambition just because I was afraid to be disappointed. The Hebrew word *pārâ* in that verse means "to bear fruit,

Pray for your To-Do List.

to grow, to increase."[2] This is the essence of ambition—it's the desire to step forward, to take risks, and expand our lives, instead of shrinking back.

For my grandmother, she wouldn't permit disappointments to be the end of her ambitions. When my grandfather decided to move the family to Lagos in the early 1960s to work as an economist in the newly independent nation of Nigeria, she found ways to use her medical skills. She volunteered at a local hospital, holding infants whose heads were flat from being left on their backs and never being held. She fed them and she bathed them. Years later, she hasn't stopped telling that story; and the impact she made there reflects her fortitude and resolve to find purposeful outlets for her ambitions. When she couldn't pursue the dream of being a doctor, it didn't hold her back from caring for others in whatever way she could. At its core, this is an expanded definition of ambition. It is pushing forward to be fruitful wherever you are (*pārâ*).

Secondary Ambitions

This means that any discussion of ambition has to recognize that <u>we hold more than one dream at a time</u>. The challenge is how to prioritize the various ambitions that you have. This is a current discussion among business leaders. They see that the Millennial generation—having lived through the dot-com bust, 9/11, and the Great Recession—have expanded their definition of ambition to include other, more personal values. A recent survey of Millennials contradicts Sandberg's assessment of women's ambition:

> Sixty-one percent (61%) see themselves as ambitious compared to 63 percent of the men. These young ambitious women are seeking ways for their professional aspirations to co-exist with their personal values. Might they actually be twice as ambitious?[3]

Having twice as many ambitions all competing for prominence is not the solution we are suggesting. We have to go back to the idea of Christian ambition. Jesus says in Matthew 6:33, "But seek first the kingdom of God and His righteousness, and all these things will be provided for you." This is an audacious promise and British theologian John Stott helps us to make some sense of how to organize our ambitions:

> Ambitions for self may be quite modest (enough to eat, to drink, and to wear as in the Sermon) or they may be grandiose (a bigger house, faster car, a higher salary, a wider reputation, more power). But whether modest or immodest, these are ambitions for myself— *my* comfort, *my* wealth, *my* status, *my* power.
>
> Ambitions for God, however, if they are to be worthy, can never be modest. There is something inherently inappropriate about cherishing small ambitions for God. How can we ever be content that he should acquire just a little more honour in the world? No. Once we are clear that God is King, then we long to see him crowned with glory and honour, and accorded his true place, which is the supreme place. We become ambitious for the spread of his kingdom and righteousness everywhere.
>
> When this is genuinely our dominant ambition, then not only will *all these things . . . be yours as well* (i.e., our material needs will be provided), but there will be no harm in having secondary ambitions, since these will be subservient to our primary ambition and not in competition with it. *Indeed it is then that secondary ambitions become healthy. Christians should be eager to develop their gifts, widen their opportunities, extend their influence and be given promotion in their work—not now to boost their own ego or build their own empire, but rather through everything they do to bring glory to God.*[4] (emphasis added)

Most conversations about ambition aren't grounded in God's glory, which means we are elevating a secondary ambition to the primary place and arguing about that. Is your job or your family most important? For believers, both are important, but both are ultimately trumped by the renown of God's name and the praise of His glory. Therefore those other ambitions must slide to second place and find their mutual contours in the redemptive purposes of the gospel.

Women should be ambitious for *everything* we see in Scripture—our jobs, callings, and our special roles as life-bearers. Even feminist Betty Friedan came to recognize the importance of this aspect of femininity some twenty years after launching the American women's movement:

> Some militants repudiated all the parts of the person-hood of women that have been and are still expressed in family, home and love. In trying to ape men's lives, they have truncated themselves away from grounding experiences. If young women lock themselves into the roles of ambitious men, I'm not sure it's a good bargain. It can be terribly imprisoning and life denying.[5]

To paraphrase John Stott's quote, Christian women should be eager to develop their gifts (husband, children, spiritual gifts) widen their opportunities (professionally and personally), extend their influence (in the church and community), and be given promotion in their work (whether paid or not), so that in everything they do they can bring glory to God. The challenge is how to juggle these secondary ambitions when they seem to be in competition with each other. We will offer some ideas in the life cycle chapters to come, offering some thoughts on how to make wise choices as you develop these secondary ambitions.

Ambitious Acts

There's a particular woman in the Bible who seemed to do an extraordinary job developing her primary ambition to magnify God's name through the secondary ambitions of her work and her marriage. Like her husband, Aquila, Priscilla was a tentmaker. According to *The Bible Background Commentary*, by this period the term *tentmaker* also applied to leatherworking in general. It was an artisan class profession, one that could be very profitable.[6]

Priscilla and Aquila both have Latin names, but we know nothing of Priscilla's origins. Perhaps she, like her husband, was from Pontus, a town on the southern coast of the Black Sea (now modern Turkey). What we do know is that they had been living in Rome until they were forced to leave by an edict of the emperor Claudius, which expelled all Jews from the city in AD 49. We also know that they moved to Corinth afterward and that's where they met the apostle Paul, who was also a tentmaker.

Their mutual labors supported all three of them and permitted them extended hours for conversation while doing their work. For months they worked and ministered together in Corinth. As was his custom, Paul went first with the gospel to the synagogue in Corinth. But when his message was rejected, he evangelized the Gentiles in Corinth and built the church that met in Priscilla's home.

At some point in their friendship, Paul says Priscilla and Aquila "risked their own necks for my life" (Rom. 16:4). This risk is not specified, but it may have occurred when Priscilla and Aquila traveled with Paul to Ephesus. Acts 19 tells us that Paul was violently opposed by Demetrius the silversmith in Ephesus, whose livelihood making silver shrines for the goddess Artemis was threatened by Paul's message.

While in Ephesus, Priscilla and Aquila met a powerful orator whose message was well-crafted but incomplete. Apollos was a Jew from Alexandria, the capital of Egypt and the home of the largest library of the ancient world. He was likely part of the Jewish aristocracy and well trained in the art of rhetoric. When Priscilla and Aquila discerned his lack of knowledge, they quietly interceded:

> A Jew named Apollos, a native Alexandrian, an
> eloquent man who was powerful in the use of the
> Scriptures, arrived in Ephesus. This man had been
> instructed in the way of the Lord; and being fervent
> in spirit, he spoke and taught the things about Jesus
> accurately, although he knew only John's baptism.
> He began to speak boldly in the synagogue. After
> Priscilla and Aquila heard him, they took him home
> and explained the way of God to him more accurately.
> (Acts 18:24–26)

It's encouraging to see how the marriage partnership of Priscilla and Aquila was lived out in their shared vocation and ministry. From these accounts, we can see that Priscilla was shaped by her primary ambition to glorify God. This led to prosperity in her work, making her wealthy enough to be a patron of the church, have a home large enough to host the young church in Ephesus, and to be able to travel with Paul. Her passion for the accuracy of the gospel message was combined with gracious wisdom, so that she knew to invite Apollos to her home and privately show him what was missing from his message. She did not embarrass him in public nor seek to make a greater name for herself by being in competition with him for influence.

Ambitions Expressed

Priscilla's ambitious example is not a dusty relic from the past. Nora and I know many women today who have similarly ambitious goals. We know women who work hard just to feed their children; and we know women who have risen in the ranks of corporations, where they lead with great skill. They are believers who work hard to represent a facet of God's character to the watching world—women whose labors are diverse in their contributions to the world around them, no matter how small or great. We have a friend whose children suffer from a rare disease and she created a foundation to raise money for research. This is unpaid work but it is vital.

We also have several friends who work for human rights organizations like the International Justice Mission, Shared Hope International, and the Jubilee Campaign because of their Godward passion for justice. We have friends who work for relief organizations like Food for the Hungry, World Vision, Doctors Without Borders, and Opportunity International because they take seriously the James 1:27 command to "look after widows and orphans in their distress." Whether paid or unpaid, these women are working hard to achieve ambitious goals for the glory of God.

Equally as important, Priscilla did not suffer from the modern "sacred/secular" divide. The whole of her life was integrated for the benefit of the gospel. Her work was a significant aspect of her mission to help the church and the Lord blessed her in it. Like Priscilla the tentmaker, modern women can be busy in fields that seem unrelated to ministry and find that God will work through their secondary ambitions to bring praise to His name. Secondary ambitions are a vital part of life and we will talk about them for the rest of the book.

Whether you are thinking about ambition in the workplace or at home, in whatever you have to do, Elisabeth Elliot's often repeated quote still rings true: "This job has been given to me to do. Therefore, it is a gift. Therefore, it is a privilege. Therefore, it is an offering I may make to God. Therefore, it is to be done gladly, if it is done for Him. Here, not somewhere else, I may learn God's way. In this job, not in some other, God looks for faithfulness."[7]

The Life Cycle of Work

Purpose, rest, identity, and ambition are concepts that shape how we work, but there's still the huge challenge of figuring out how to do that in each stage of life. In the final section of this book, we try to apply these and other biblical concepts to the seasons of growing up, launching into adulthood, balancing family and career, managing others, and entering the "open nest" time.

We have included several stories of our own in these chapters, as well as those of other women we know. It can be helpful to see how others have applied wisdom principles to their lives, but these limited illustrations are not offered as one-size-fits-all examples. They are merely illustrative of how some women have thought about the modern challenges of productivity and success, and how they worked out solutions fitting their individual circumstances, gifts, capacities, and responsibilities.

While we hope you find these ideas helpful, we are more eager to consistently remind you that God is not surprised by the challenges we face today in being productive at home and work. He willingly and generously gives His wisdom to all who ask Him in faith (James 1:5). That's the overall theme for this final section of the book.

CHAPTER 9

Growing Up

I come from a long line of List Makers. My family had lists for every-thing—from household chores and what to pack for vacations, to my mother's "Honey-Do List" for my father. That particular list resided on the chalkboard in the kitchen. This list actually contained entire projects, not just tasks, and as a result it had a semipermanent status in the kitchen.

One day my father finally finished one of his long-lasting projects: painting the fence. I had been outside "helping" him and as he put the lids on the cans of stain, I raced inside to triumphantly scratch that item off the list. A few minutes later, he entered the kitchen and looked with dismay at the chalkboard. Protesting my impulsive action, he picked up the eraser, wiped off that crossed-off task, and wrote it all over again. Just to cross it off again—by himself.

"That was *my* accomplishment," he sternly reminded me, before breaking into a small smile. "*You* don't cross things off of *my* list!"

That was the day I realized the joy of accomplishment—even if it wasn't my own.

Accomplishment is the psychological reward for hard work. Money is the tangible reward for hard work. Godly influence is the spiritual reward for hard work. All three are important for children to learn at a young age, and that's the focus of this chapter. While we thoroughly expect that for this chapter the vast majority of readers will be parents, we applaud any girl curious enough about her future to read the words of advice we have for you at the end.

Instructions for Wise Living

One of the first lessons children need to learn about work is that productivity matters to God. What we forget, though, is that this starts with us, not them. They learn from what they see adults model.

We see this in the book of Proverbs, a book of wisdom from a parent to a child. Proverbs emphasizes that it offers knowledge and instruction to the young and inexperienced, with the assumption that the parents live up to the same standards. Throughout this collection of sayings for the wise, we find consistent warnings about laziness.

> Go to the ant, you slacker! Observe its ways and become wise. Without leader, administrator, or ruler, it prepares its provisions in summer; it gathers its food during harvest. How long will you stay in bed, you slacker? When will you get up from your sleep? A little sleep, a little slumber, a little folding of the arms to rest, and your poverty will come like a robber, your need, like a bandit. (Prov. 6:6–11)

> Idle hands make one poor, but diligent hands bring riches. The son who gathers during summer is prudent; the son who sleeps during harvest is disgraceful. (Prov. 10:4–5)

> The one who works his land will have plenty of food, but whoever chases fantasies lacks sense. (Prov. 12:11)

> The slacker craves, yet has nothing, but the diligent is fully satisfied. (Prov. 13:4)

> Do you see a man skilled in his work? He will stand in the presence of kings. He will not stand in the presence of unknown men. (Prov. 22:29)

The assumption Solomon makes is that parents model productivity, not laziness, and then teach this virtue to their children. When children are very young, they like to imitate the work that their parents do. Unfortunately this interest and enthusiasm seems to peak when their skills are the weakest. Once children become old enough to become semi-proficient in the tasks, they lose that natural initiative.

They have discovered that work can be hard.

I have clear memories of following my father around in late summer evenings "helping" him mow our lawn. I'm sure I was more annoying than helpful, a distraction to the task at hand. When I was hanging out *imitating* work with my father, I had fun. As soon as I was proficient enough to mow the lawn on my own, it had lost its charm. I had discovered the thorns and thistles of Paradise Lost . . . and I was disenchanted.

Parents should not only model good work patterns, but also take the long view when training children to understand the value of work. The most important part is to begin at home when young children are more willing to work than they are skilled. At first these tasks won't be done the way you prefer, but the goal is not to have a perfectly clean house or manicured lawn. The goal is to train your children to work. Applaud their efforts to help, even when they are subpar. Their skills will catch up one day.

Rearing children to understand the value of hard work is hard work in and of itself. It requires repetition, consistency, and determination. By doing this we are setting an example of hard work done in faith. Even in small ways, such as training children to put away toys, parents are setting up an expectation that children contribute simply because they exist in the household. Parenting doesn't mean doing all the work for them. As Proverbs points out, it is about training children to spurn laziness and work hard to please God.

Working Together

Pam had four young children when she was introduced to a line of children's books that captured her interest. She came home from a book show with a sense that selling these books was something she could pursue as a home-based business while rearing her children. She had a personal interest in reading and in promoting children's literacy. After talking with her husband, Bob, she launched her own company to sell these books to libraries, schools, and families.

At the time, her oldest child, Michael, was eleven and her youngest was two. As the company grew, so did her family. She had her fifth child while building the business. But from the start, everyone worked in it and everyone benefited from it. "They were very happily involved; they loved the books," Pam recalls. "My children were my best spokespeople for the products."

"We thought what our mom was doing looked like a lot of fun and we wanted to help where we could," Michael says. The children learned to update customer contacts, printed and assembled newsletters, prepped packages and letters, assisted with inventory, and even traveled with Pam to the curriculum fairs. Later on, Michael put his interest in computers to work and developed a website for the business.

Eventually, the children also developed their own small businesses. Michael and his brother, Sean, started by selling bags that removed Christmas trees without scattering the tree needles everywhere. Bob ordered the bags and fronted the cash. The boys went door-to-door selling them and kept the profits after paying back their father. Michael also started a lawn business, in which all of his younger brothers eventually participated. His youngest brother still has some of the same customers twenty years later.

Pam says that the business only worked well with the support of the whole family. Bob was very involved the first four years in what Pam was doing. He was the ideas person, developing various sales and growth strategies. He also helped her put parameters in place to keep the business from overtaking family life. At one point, they even questioned putting a hold on the company due to the demands of both a growing family and a growing business.

To make it work, Pam and Bob required the children to contribute to the household. "A tip from another mother revolutionized my life: teach your kids to do their own laundry," Pam says. "From that point on, we expected that they do their laundry once a week."

Pam's business was quite successful, contributing a significant amount to the family budget, paying for her children's private high school tuition, and ultimately for her children's college education—supplementing the scholarships that they earned. Her three oldest children are now married with families of their own and successful careers. As adults, they have repeatedly thanked their parents for teaching them the value of work and requiring them to earn and budget their money. "That initiative and diligence they instilled in us long ago continues to benefit us and our employers," Michael says.

Many would look at Pam's experience with wonder and ask: *How did she do it all?* But Pam is quick to point out that she *didn't* do it all. Her job running the home was not to run herself ragged doing it all, but to manage the home and direct the work of the children living there. The same principle applied to her business.

"It would be honest to say that there were some days that felt too full, and even chaotic, but overall we—the whole family—were in agreement to make this business work," Pam says. "If chaos had become a pattern, I believe Bob and I would have agreed to end the business."

Even now, her adult children and their spouses talk of creating a family business that the extended family could run together. "To this day, we still think about what family business we could get *all* involved in. That would be a blast," Pam says.

Talent Management

God gives parents insight into their children and how they work. Some children find it much harder to work and learn, and require more teaching and attention. God not only calls us to model hard work, but to patiently teach our children in the ways that strengthen them. Parents have to be humble with the process of teaching children how to work hard.

In the business world, this is thought of as "talent management." It is a crucial part of parenting to identify specific, natural skills that children possess and then use that knowledge to teach and motivate them. For example, are they motivated by praise? By a monetary reward? By a promise of a special experience? Use the insights God gives you about your children's personalities to reward their work in a way that appeals to them.

On the flip side, it is also essential for parents to teach their children about their natural weaknesses. I (Nora) have a friend whose son really struggles with math and she says it's hard to see her son come home feeling less intelligent than his friends in class. As parents, we have a responsibility not only to praise our children's strengths, but also to remind our children that no one is good at everything. In a culture that often spurns humility, godly parents can train their children to realize that sometimes we just have to admit our weaknesses and work harder at some things than others.

Remember my (Carolyn) pony story from the ambition chapter? When my dad read an early draft of that chapter, he remarked that back then he didn't realize my annoying tenacity could be a good thing to cultivate and properly direct.

"It was just plain vexing at the time," he said with a soft laugh. "I didn't have any problem with you wanting a pony. I thought it was rather admirable. But the *reality* of having a pony was the frustrating part. You didn't understand that having a horse was a very big responsibility for an adult, much less a child."

My father may regret his lack of foresight, but God made sure I eventually learned the reality check I needed. Now we both see that this tenacious ambition was a necessary trait that I would need to start businesses as an adult. Granted, some of those ventures would have been more successful if I had learned earlier that I needed a reality check. I could have benefitted from a better understanding of my strengths and weaknesses.

Better than a Cookie

According to the published history of the Girl Scouts, nearly 100 years ago the Mistletoe Troop in Muskogee, Oklahoma, first baked cookies and sold them in its high school cafeteria as a service project. But soon after, it became a fundraising opportunity for the troop. Today the Girl Scouts promote cookie sales as a way for girls to learn five important life skills: goal-setting, decision-making, money management, people skills, and business ethics. That's why the cookies are not sold online.

But good intentions don't always play out. As I was writing this chapter, I was solicited to buy some of those delicious cookies. By a parent. Of course I placed my order, but then I gently inquired why the Girl Scout herself didn't pitch me. I was told she was too busy. Unlike scouting back in the day, I was informed, the Girl Scout Council now instructs the girls to never go door-to-door to sell cookies, but only to sell to friends and family. With a 100-box quota, parents are forced to help the girls meet the goal.

Parents selling cookies undermines the whole point, of course. I don't say that unsympathetically. I recognize there are times when you have to pick your battles as a parent, focusing on one area at a time with each child, or there are seasons in your own life when you are maxed out in your personal capacities and can't take on one more family activity. In the case of these particular Girl Scout cookies, my mom friend is the troop leader and had the obligation to raise money for the troop. Her daughter is a junior in high school and taking a very hard course load. Given the multitude of responsibilities, this mother is helping her daughter be strategic. She felt the number of boxes of cookies her daughter might sell isn't as important as her school work.

We commend this mother for placing an appropriate emphasis on education. Parents are incredibly influential in the success of a child's education. A recent study reports that parental involvement is a more significant factor in a child's academic performance than the qualities of the school itself.[1] While we recognize that education isn't the ultimate measure of success, the statistics are clear on the benefits of education. According to a recent U.S. Census Bureau survey, the median salary of an individual who has only a high-school diploma is $27,967, whereas an individual with a bachelor's degree is $47,345.[2] While not everyone can afford college, this shows that there are long-lasting implications for pursuing and excelling in education.

This is a stewardship issue for most Americans, where we can take our education system for granted. An advocate for the global right to free education writes that those fortunate enough to live in nations where compulsory education is free tend to think that this is the case worldwide.[3] But it's not. There are a number of developing nations where families have to pay school fees for primary education. That has led to 69 million children worldwide not being in school, mostly in sub-Saharan Africa and Southern Asia. The United Nations (UN) has made achieving universal primary education as one of its Millennial Development Goals, to be achieved by 2015. While substantial progress has been made, the UN admits that the current pace of progress is insufficient to meet this goal.[4]

That's why it's good stewardship to encourage your children to pursue their education. It shouldn't be about the numbers—the grades, the awards, the badges, or boxes of cookies sold. In a society obsessed with performance, it is important to help children to see the real value of learning. Turning the discussion around from achievement to a godly pursuit of excellence gives the argument for education some biblical teeth. It also teaches them that one of the ways they learn to work is to work at becoming educated.

These illustrations (positive and negative) aren't meant to pile on more condemnation about what you are or are not doing as a parent. They are offered merely to make us *all* stop and think about how purposeful we are in training the next generation about the value of work. Even if you don't have children of your own, you are still part of this process. You can get involved in formal tutoring programs, volunteer to help a friend's child with homework, or support a girl's education in a developing nation through various poverty relief organizations.

For parents, the point is that you have a responsibility to train your child, but you are not doing this on your own. Whether you have to motivate your child or rein in her pony-sized ambitions, only the Holy Spirit can ensure the fruit in your child's life. The Lord is very patient with us, working over the whole of our lives. He is doing the same with your child. He will prove Himself faithful to both of you.

For Girls

This last section is an overview for you girls. We hope that you are reading this because you want to begin to understand why productivity is so important for women. It is merely an overview, but we trust this section will give you a place to start understanding why work matters, even at a young age.

We're going to borrow from the Girl Scouts because they break down some important life skills into some great practical categories like: goal-setting, decision-making, money management, people skills, and business ethics. Before we get into them, though, we'd like to add one more category: purpose. Just like adults, it is most important to know the reason why we work. We need to know our purpose in work.

God made work to be a good thing, but our sin makes it hard. But God gives us a promise: as we follow Him, and try to become more like Him, He renews us in His image, and also renews our work. He can take our work and turn it into something that glorifies Him and shows His love to others.

We need to do the work with a bigger purpose than just getting the job done: we want to be so skilled in the work that we will be invited to stand in the presence of kings (Prov. 22:29). Another Scripture says that we, as daughters, should be "like corner pillars that are carved in the palace style" (Ps. 144:12). Whatever we do, we want to make sure that our work is not only done well, but that it is work fitting of a palace. People practiced in leisure do not stand in the presence of kings or have the strength to hold up a palace. Our purpose is to fulfill God's design for us to work, but to do it in a way that brings God glory.

Now, let's get back to the Girl Scout cookies—oops, their principles, of course. (We wish we were eating Thin Mints out of the freezer with you right now!)

Goal Setting: Do you set goals? What motivates you? Are you motivated by praise? By a monetary reward? By a special experience? Use the insights God gives you about yourself, and things you learn about yourself from others, to set goals with rewards that mean something to you. Start by making a list of your priorities, such as: God, family, school, church and personal, then ask an adult who knows you well to help you set goals.

Remember that we never work as hard for something we don't want. We work a lot harder for what we really do want. But it isn't just about rewards every time. External motivation eventually needs to become an internal motivation—such as crossing off an item on a checklist or mastering a new skill. We have to learn how to do the work, like cleaning our room, because it's the right thing to do.

We also need to learn that one particular goal is often a collection of smaller tasks with their own goals—and that effective time management is a big part of reaching a goal. We have to learn to break down the big goal into smaller tasks with a time line of completion. Whether the goal is learning how to make a cake or getting a top grade on a special project, project management is a learned skill. Don't wait for the night before your science fair project is due to learn how to break down larger tasks into smaller, manageable ones.

Decision Making: Everyone needs help making decisions. Even now, I (Nora) at thirty-three (gasp!) still call my mom to talk things through. No matter what age you are, girls like to talk about it. We need help understanding and applying biblical wisdom; we can't do it alone! Left to ourselves, some of us would never commit because we're scared; and others of us just plunge ahead and land in a pile of trouble. Talking it out helps. If you can visualize and describe what you expect will happen, it can help you to understand. Sometimes you'll make bad decisions, but that will teach you a lesson too. Like the time my mom let my sister ruin an entire batch of cookies, so that she'd learn not to wing a recipe. It's important to read the directions so that you don't mistake a half-teaspoon for a half-cup of salt!

My friend, Lauren, has a good motto for good decision making: "Do what you *have* to do, so you can do what you *want* to do." She tells her eight-year-old son to make wise decisions about what he'll do after school, to ensure he has some time for fun. In addition to getting his homework done, he knows he has to feed and clean up behind the dogs, get the mail, and clear the dinner table before he can play. He sometimes negotiates with his mom, but he has to make his own decisions. We have to learn to make good decisions based on the goals we set!

Money Management: This is a biggie. The temptation to spend a lot of money is so hard for us girls. We've all experienced the little pit-in-our-stomach moment after we've stepped outside the store with things we don't really need. Relying on the right clothes, shoes, and cosmetic products won't make us really happy; it's so short-lived, because there will be something else new to get tomorrow.

Unfortunately, those habits don't leave you once you turn twenty. You need help learning how to create good habits now. Have you ever made a budget? Try to set up an amount of money you can use for discretionary (another word for things you want, but don't essentially need) items and stick to it. Money management is a skill that every girl needs. We need to learn basic financial skills like how to comparison shop, balance a checkbook, manage credit, and save for the future.

One recent study said that American parents spend about one-third less time talking with their children about how to handle money than parents in other countries.⁵ Have you ever talked with your parents about money? You don't have to know everything that goes in and out of your parents' bank accounts, but by talking about it with them, you might learn about how they save and spend their money.

It's not just about the $20 that you spend, though, but also about the $20 that you could save. Saving money for the long-term doesn't seem that important now, but imagine if you just save $20 a month from babysitting jobs. Twenty dollars might seem like a little, but by the time you are thirty, you could have $5,000. Compounding interest, which is a fancy way of saying how money makes more money for you, is a way that takes little amounts of money and makes them into dreams come true—like buying a car.

People Skills: We can sum this up as "Teenage Drama—Just Say No." In fact, most of the hard lessons adult women have to learn when they start working could be overcome if they had learned how to respond to relationship drama as a teenager. Drama is shorthand for what the Bible calls "fear of man." It is living for the opinion of others, either in fearing rejection or craving approval. While there is a learning curve to attaining this kind of maturity, we encourage you girls to put the opinions of others in perspective—everyone from the school bully to the prom queen is captive to this problem. True confidence in God is expressed in humility, especially in conflict, a willingness to hear from others, gratitude for what you have received, empathy toward outsiders, and a willingness to ask questions for clarity when you are confused when people give you mixed signals.

When you're younger, people skills are learning to say things like "Hi" and "Thank you." As you get older, it is learning how to engage with an adult in conversation, learning to compete in sports with respect for others, and, probably the most difficult, learning to resolve conflict with your friends.

Finally, to create solid people skills, you need to learn about other cultures and experiences. If you have friends from a different culture, ask them about it and try to grow in respect for the way other people do things or read books about it. As we worked on this book, a brave teenage girl named Malala Yousafzai was shot by the Taliban in Pakistan for promoting education for girls. Watch some videos about her and other girls like her, to learn that even teens can stand up to injustice and be heard.

Business Ethics: The Girl Scouts use this phrase, but as Christians, ethics is about developing a character shaped by God's Word. Don't lie, don't cheat, say thank you to those who help you, keep your promises, show up when you say you will, do your work in a timely way, respond to people who contact you, and so forth are all examples of having character in your work ethic.

One of the most practical things you can do as a young woman is keeping a schedule. Having integrity means that you commit your time and you keep your promises. Whether you use a calendar, or an app on your phone, or a list at home, you are responsible for keeping up on your commitments. At some point or another, we all make mistakes—we forget that quiz or we get sick when we are supposed to babysit, but by making and keeping a schedule, you develop a work ethic that honors God and others.

Learning to discern other people's integrity is almost as important as having integrity of your own. A simple measurement to use is that if a person has anything hidden or secretive that is not exposed to the light (God and others), it's probably questionable and lacks integrity. This applies to friends who make bad choices, but it also applies to your relationships with adults.

What if a manipulative youth pastor wants to "have a special relationship" with you that needs to be nurtured in secret? Or when your boss wants you to keep quiet about the money he takes on the side in cash at the restaurant where you're working? It also applies to the "modeling agent" who approaches you at the mall and tells you to come to a private photo shoot in his home.

This is a hard lesson to learn, but so necessary. No matter what justification people give for the context of hidden activity, you need to understand that righteous activity does not need to hide in secret. But what happens if a friend wants you to keep a heavy secret and swear you to silence? It's better not to make the promise of silence to receive a confidence, because the situation of the secret may actually require action. If you are told about abuse or other issues that have legal consequences, you will have to tell an adult. Or it may be something very serious you can't process on your own without counsel. Often, however, the secret is gossip and the person relaying it needs to be directed to a solution that does not involve spreading rumors.

Girls, we applaud you for reading this! We want you to understand how excited we are that you want to learn to be a woman who loves God and follows His ways, especially as it applies to productivity. We are cheering you on and are excited to see what happens when you put these principles to work!

Final Words

For girls and women alike, the illustrations in this chapter aren't meant to pile on more condemnation about what you are or are not doing. They are offered merely to make us all stop and think about how purposeful we are in training the next generation to be productive. Whether you are young or old, you are still part of this legacy. As parents and mentors, and as children and mentees, we need to participate in growing together, to learn how we can work productively together.

Be encouraged that you are not doing this on your own. Isaiah 40:11 (ESV) says, "He will tend his flock like a shepherd; he will gather the lambs in his arms; he will carry them in his bosom, and gently lead those that are with young." God promises to shepherd His people. The Lord is very patient with us, guiding the whole of our lives. He is doing the same with our children.

CHAPTER 10

Launching to Adulthood

"*What do you want to be when you grow up?*"

All your life, you've heard the same question from adults. At four, you may have confidently stated you wanted to be a ballerina or perhaps an astronaut. At fourteen, you may have secretly hoped to be a pop singer or a renowned surgeon. But no matter your dreams, you lived life in lockstep with your peers, moving through life largely at the same intervals.

But as you launch into adulthood, the predictable benchmarks disappear. It becomes harder to discern what success looks like—and if you are measuring up.

What do I want to be when I grow up? Decades later, I'm still trying to figure that one out. One of my earliest memories is writing a short play, rounding up my friends and directing the production, and then taking it from house to house, charging my neighbors to watch on their front porches. That's not too far from what I do today—professionally, I ended up as a writer and director. But that's only part of the answer. I wanted to be other things, too, like a wife and mother, a compassionate friend, a good cook, and maybe even a certified scuba diver.

How do you benchmark *those* goals? If your friends reach them first, does that mean you are failing or got left behind? What if you change your mind along the way? Is that allowed?

When I was hired for my first job, my father took me aside to give me an important insight. "Carolyn, you are motivated by gold stars, high grades, and lots of regular feedback," he said. "But you won't get that at work. Don't expect praise for merely doing what you were hired to do. If you keep getting paid, you will know you are doing a good job."

Welcome to adulthood. You have many important choices to make, more decisions than we could possibly address, in fact. So in this chapter, we will explore eight concepts that will give you a solid foundation for successful productivity as a young woman.

1. Plan Ahead

As we see it, the choices you make now will affect the trajectory of your productivity over the coming decades. What can be hard to anticipate at this stage is that you have to plan ahead for the dualities you might face being a woman who is fruitful in childrearing and economically productive in an era when those two things are often done in different places. The emotionally challenging aspect of this is that you have to cultivate faith in God so that you neither presume on your future nor fear what may come. Fortunately, Scripture directs us how to think about our future plans:

> Come now, you who say, "Today or tomorrow we will
> travel to such and such a city and spend a year there
> and do business and make a profit." You don't even
> know what tomorrow will bring—what your life will
> be! For you are like smoke that appears for a little
> while, then vanishes. Instead, you should say, "If the
> Lord wills, we will live and do this or that." But as it
> is, you boast in your arrogance. All such boasting is
> evil. (James 4:13–16)

You see here that James is not busting on the person who has a plan. He is merely correcting the one who has arrogantly put all his *confidence* in that plan. Planning ahead is good, but it has to be done with humble understanding that everything is subject to God's will.

So it is with how you anticipate your future. From all the women we have talked to for this book, not once did we hear someone say, "My life has turned out *exactly* how I expected it would." But from my midlife vantage point, I can confidently assure you that there will be many more blessings than you anticipate and many more trials. But through it all, God's grace will be triumphant. Of that, I am most assuredly confident.

For now, most of you will need to plan ahead for the duality of life—how do I support myself now and into the future? What if I add a husband and children to this life? What if I don't and I remain single? Is my profession something I can scale down if needed when I have a family, and then I can return to it later? What are the implications of debt on my future choices? Ask yourself these questions to test your assumptions, but hold your future expectations loosely.

Some of the most frustrated women I know are the ones who did not do this multi-track planning when they were younger. Women who never expected to remain single into their thirties are full of cautionary tales about their lack of planning to have a flourishing career, retirement savings, and a home of their own. They regret the years they were stuck on hold as young women, waiting for something that hasn't yet materialized. On the other hand, women who have the powerhouse careers in their thirties but never thought about how to incorporate families are overwhelmed when children come along.

So make your plans, but do a lot of market research as you go. Ask people in the field you are considering for an informational interview, then inquire of them what their work-life balance has been like and what advice they would give you. Find out from your business and personal contacts alike what they wish they had done differently as young adults. Read widely in your field, following social media and trade publications alike. Ask your family and friends for their counsel about your personal strengths and weaknesses.

Then pray. All your best research will only lead you to come up with a plan that *might* prove profitable, just as James says. But prayer will keep you seeking the Lord about those plans, and that humble dependence upon Him prevents the proud boasting that James condemns.

But what if you are not the Type A confidently-making-plans personality, but rather you are someone who often wrestles with making a decision at all?

Romans 14:23 has a life verse for you—for all of us, in fact: "For whatever does not proceed from faith is sin." That's the ESV translation. The HCSB version translates it as, "everything that is not from a conviction is sin." In other words, if you do something to please other people, or because you fear their reaction, or because it makes you look better—or for any other reason than because you have faith that this decision or act pleases God and it is His provision for you—then you are sinning, plain and simple. Your ambitions are for something other than God's glory.

This is really important. No matter your temperament, you will be tested in nearly *every* way possible in your future decisions. If you aren't grounded in this important biblical principle, you will flounder—either unable to make a decision or regretting one you made for all the wrong reasons. Be firmly anchored in this truth as you move forward in life, and you will be spared a lot of heartache.

2. Know Your Focal Point

Whenever my mother would put extra effort into her appearance, she would say she was "getting gussied up." According to one dictionary, the first known use of that slang phrase was from 1952.[1] It could have been made popular by the flamboyant tennis star of that era, Gussie Moran.

In 1949, Gussie Moran decided to create a name for herself at the prestigious Wimbledon championship in England—but not through her tennis skills. She used her racy, lace-trimmed underwear peeking out from her short skirt to do it. Photographers would lie down on the grass court to get the panty shot. Dubbed "Gorgeous Gussie," her wardrobe choices caused the officials at Wimbledon and the U.S. Open to clamp down with new wardrobe rules. She later wore more sedate garb at the U.S. Open. "I know I will disappoint the crowd, but I can't concentrate on my game when people are staring at my panties," she said.[2]

Three years later, Gussie Moran retired from competitive tennis. She died at age eighty-nine, having spent her final years alone and in poverty. Tennis journalist Bud Collins said, "I think she was saddened that her tennis wasn't the focus, rather than her bottom and her legs."

The moral of the story is what you make the focus about yourself will be your reputation and your legacy, so choose wisely. At this stage in your life, you are likely to be at your physical peak. You are also living in a sexual culture where fashion reflects that aesthetic—flesh is everywhere. So you have to decide where you will draw attention.

You want your skills and character to be front and center, not your body. Modesty is not just a protection against sexual sin; it is a protection of your assets at work. As you consider this, know that when you make your sexuality your focal point, you are typically dismissed as a serious player in almost any work environment because you are a distraction. Shaunti Feldhahn is an author who has made a career out of surveying men and women to help us understand our basic differences. In one study that she conducted, when a female presenter was showing cleavage while giving a four-point talk, the percentage of men who remembered her four points dropped by 25 percent.[3]

Men assume women know and understand what they are doing when they dress in revealing ways. Feeling manipulated because of the visual distraction, many men view their female colleagues who dress this way with less respect. "The woman is seen as less than business savvy, even immaturely trying to create a business advantage by making the meeting about sexual attraction," Feldhahn writes. She goes on to quote a senior executive who said: "It creates a barrier immediately if a woman comes into a meeting showing cleavage. A woman has to get to the point where she realizes this isn't about sex, it's about business. Showing cleavage won't necessarily kill the deal, but it absolutely makes me question her judgment."[4]

This is not the same as making your femininity known. The International Monetary Fund's (IMF) first female managing director received this advice from her mother: *be attractive, but not seductive.* As head of the IMF, Christine Lagarde knows that her words can rock global markets. One newspaper article said Lagarde is classically French in her femininity but makes her competence the world's focal point:

> Several men described her elegance as important but did not want that to sound leering or sexist; several women cited the same quality but insisted they didn't want to sound silly or frivolous. The bright scarves she chooses, the gold earrings she designs with a jeweler friend, the floral and intoxicating Hermes perfume she wears ("Un Jardin sur le Nil") are seen as grace notes that add up to something. "It's not just about the Chanel dress; it's about how you handle yourself in the dress," [former Congresswoman Jane] Harman said. "She delivers messages in a way that people hear them. She's not whiny or scratchy."[5]

Lagarde has made some unconventional motherhood choices, but her reserved femininity in a global leadership role is worth consideration. As Feldhahn quotes one corporate executive: "Women have the ability to be completely beautiful and completely appropriate."[6]

We emphasize modesty because we think that your skills should be the focal point. As a young woman, you are still developing your professional identity and the reputation that will precede as you move up in your career.

3. Pay Your Dues

When you land your first full-time job, it's imperative that you understand you have been hired to fill a position on a team that has one critical mission: to make and sustain the organization's profitability. You have a role to play in this mission, but it's not the starring role. In fact, you have to prove yourself to the rest of the team that you are worthy of that role. It's called paying your dues. To that end, you need to know that no one really cares about how fulfilled you are—or are not—in this role. It's not about you, but about the organization.

Though my film company is very small, it's not unusual that I receive unsolicited résumés. Most come with sincere letters explaining how much the applicant likes film, how the applicant grew up watching film, and how the applicant loves to travel, and how filmmaking can provide that opportunity.

Honestly, I dismiss those letters right away. Don't tell me how a job at my company can fulfill all your dreams. Tell me why I need you for my critical mission. Then I will know you understand the big picture and that you might make a significant contribution. Your goal with any new job is to figure out how to add value. Know exactly how your position contributes to the company's bottom line.

Be prepared. If you don't know, ask informed questions, but only after you have done some research. Never ask busy people questions that you have not researched. I repeat: *Don't make other people do your homework*. Those of us who were already working when the digital age arrived marvel at the wealth of information available through "the interwebs." Fire up your keyboard and do your homework so that you can come up with the one really insightful question that proves your worth simply because you figured out what was valuable to ask.

One more vitally important tip: Respond. As in, respond to your e-mails. Respond to your phone calls. Respond to your invitations. Never think it's a good idea to ignore your boss, your clients, or your colleagues. Or anyone who is trying to throw a party, plan a wedding, or invite you to dinner, for that matter. It doesn't matter if you "don't do e-mail" or you "don't like talking on the phone." Get a response back in a timely manner because it honors others' work and time. These few practices will show that you understand the process of paying your dues and will help you move up in an organization.

4. Play Your Position

Just like every great team sport, you need to know your role. Where do you fit? Who calls the plays? How does the team work? Your role is to add value to the company. The key person to evaluate that contribution? Your boss.

Make it your aim to know exactly what factors go into the valuation. Don't assume you know unless you have asked important questions such as: What is the measure of success for my position? What are my key deliverables? What are the delivery milestones I need to hit? In what format and how often do you want feedback from me? (Some bosses want verbal reports, some want written reports. Some want daily updates. Some want weekly updates. Know which your boss wants.) With this information, when it comes time to review your performance and (hopefully) negotiate a pay raise, you will be able to discuss concrete facts about what you achieved.

This is not easy. There are many people in middle management who struggle to lead in a clear and effective manner. I (Nora) have worked for several difficult bosses. One was disengaged from her team, another was a weak leader and, yet another, was a moody micromanager. My goal with each of them was to sell myself as a team player, no matter what I thought about their management style.

This isn't the same thing as kissing up. There are biblical principles at work, like those described in Proverbs 25:15: "A ruler can be persuaded through patience, and a gentle tongue can break a bone." By demonstrating hard work and teamwork, many a difficult boss can be won over, even if their demands and style could wear you down.

As corporate structures become increasingly team-focused, it becomes imperative that you know your position well. This involves understanding your responsibilities and following through on your commitments. If you are unclear about your work assignments, don't be afraid to ask for the information you need. Just don't whine about the workload, unless it is unjust and prolonged.

Playing your position also means "playing well with others." Just like you probably learned in kindergarten, this idea is vital to your success in the workplace. Relationships aren't always easy. But don't ignore who your coworkers are and their needs. Ask them questions and serve them. Just don't succumb to playing the game of office politics. One of the most dangerous things you can do is to participate in unchecked gossip with others; it endangers your job and your Christian witness.

I (Nora) have seen the negative effects of gossip on a workplace and how quickly it leads to disharmony on a team. Through different cycles of bosses, I tried to encourage my coworkers to talk about how we could solve problems together, rather than just add to the gossip mill.

Another way that you can play your part is by serving others. This doesn't mean doing all their work, it means caring for them as people. There are bound to be some people you get along well with, and there are others you will have to work harder at treating with the dignity and respect they deserve. The effort is worth it for two reasons: 1) it shows you are a team player, and 2) it's a way to demonstrate the love of Christ at your job.

5. Get to the Point

One of my first jobs was working for a Fortune 50 company in the Washington, D.C., public relations office. I was totally at the bottom of the food chain, I was clueless about the importance of hierarchy, and I had no idea that my only role was to shut up and listen. My boss's boss was the executive vice president of communications, a direct report to the CEO. Our division had an unusually short chain of command in that large multinational company. All of which set me up for being at a dinner on a business trip with my boss and his boss where I showed my immaturity by talking too much. I didn't pick up on any of the signals until the EVP made it really clear what I was supposed to do. Turning to me, he cut me off mid-anecdote by saying, "Would you shut the (bleep) up?"

I've heard variations of that request over the years, though none that blunt. So let me spare you the same experience. Here's a tip that will make you far more effective in all your interactions with men, both in your romantic relationships and on the job: *Get to the point.* Nearly all of your communications will benefit from getting to your point quickly. Your listeners can always ask for more details if they are interested, but if you frontload your conversation with too many details, you will generally incite frustration and impatience.

"The way many of the men I interviewed described it, they prefer the conclusion or the bottom line up front because it helps them listen," Feldhahn writes. "Without it, they find it more difficult to absorb the information. One executive explained, 'There's something about a male brain that wants the end of the story so he knows why he's listening.'"

Second, when you are asked a question, answer the specific question. Don't skip ahead to answer *what you think* men want to know. You may be completely wrong in assuming you know why he is asking. You will head off a lot of conflicts if you answer with the facts pertaining to that one question first. I still battle that tendency, but at least I am aware of my weakness. I have caused a lot of unnecessary conflict because I skipped ahead to where I thought someone was going in their line of questioning and responded either defensively (never a helpful position to take) or confusingly.

While this might be a masculine tendency, in my observation it serves busy people of both genders. Time is the most precious commodity in the workforce because it's the only resource you can't renew. Profits can be restored, people can be replaced, but the passing of time is relentless.

6. Address Conflict

In one job I held my boss expected the work to be done on time, on budget, and with exceptional character. Make your deadline and budget and apologize later was my mode of operation when I started.

Do you want to hazard a guess about one of my biggest on-the-job lessons? Yep, conflict resolution. When performance, reputation, budgets, and deadlines are all in the mix with your colleagues, you can count on experiencing conflict.

The first thing you need to know about conflict on the job is that you don't need to take it personally. Most of the time, you are having a conflict about a process, a task, or a function. This is not about you as a person, as much as it may feel that way. Keep your reactions (and later thoughts about them) contained around the particular issue and not the history of everything that's ever happened. This can be a particular challenge for women, as we generally are more relational than men, but it is vital we compartmentalize conflict to specific situations or examples.

The second thing you need to know is the gospel really empowers and equips us with the words and framework we need to confront people and achieve resolution. In fact, the conflict-resolution process outlined in Matthew 18 is exactly the process you need at work.

> If your brother sins against you, go and tell him his
> fault, between you and him alone. If he listens to you,
> you have gained your brother. But if he does not lis-
> ten, take one or two others along with you, that every
> charge may be established by the evidence of two or
> three witnesses. If he refuses to listen to them, tell it
> to the church. (Matt. 18:15–17 ESV)

The point is, go to those who have offended you private and directly. Go with a genuine desire to understand their views and see the breach healed. Go asking questions, with the assumption you could be wrong. If you can't reconcile on your own, get the next appropriate people involved. At work, this may be your boss or your human resources director, as appropriate. The point is, only involve those who are or could be part of the solution. Then if that doesn't work, you must appeal to the larger authority. But it should begin with the private conversation. Adding it to the gossip mill around the office, even to your best bud at work, is not seeking a biblical solution, nor does it protect your job.

What can be hard to understand is that, at times, conflict is a gift to you from your loving Father. It can expose your own weaknesses that He wants to correct. That is never comfortable, especially when weaknesses in the office are public. But if handled properly, conflict can lead to reconciliation and stronger working relationships. Our natural tendencies to either go on the attack to defend ourselves or to retreat to protect ourselves never fare well. It takes calm courage to call out conflict, but it can produce amazing results.

My friend Christine once called me because she was experiencing conflict at work and was frustrated by the lack of respect she received from her colleagues. She was a team leader among peers—one of the most delicate leadership situations to pull off. While her bosses and clients regularly praised her work, she was often criticized by her colleagues behind the scenes and made to feel incompetent. In meetings she would be talked over and cut off in conversation, and her ideas were dismissed. She would be openly criticized by her peers and undermined by her own team, despite working to achieve consensus. The junior level employees followed the example of the team and would regularly make condescending comments. Worst of all, this was done by those she was supposed to lead. After a while Christine hated coming to work. Her authority was crippled, her colleagues didn't respect her, and she didn't know how to improve the situation.

I encouraged Christine to speak up and address the situation with her colleagues. She owed it to her employer not to let this negative dynamic continue, as it was undermining productivity. In keeping with the initial private conversation approach in Matthew 18, I suggested she schedule a coffee or private meeting with each of her colleagues and open her meeting with an appropriate affirmation: "I'm excited that we have this project and your skills as a [whatever] are important for our success." But then she needed to get to the problem at hand in a non-threatening, warm, and confident manner that she could pull off: "But I wonder if I have offended you? Because it seems that I might have, based on X situation. What is your take on this?" After receiving an answer, Christine should make sure that the other person knows she is confident it can be resolved because they want the same results: "I'm sure we can work this out. I'm confident we can make our team successful."

I also cautioned Christine to remember that it's likely neither side is completely right. Remembering this makes it easier to own your junk— the contributions you made to the conflict at hand. Entrust the other person's reactions to the Lord. You can't control how they will react, but you have done what you could to be at peace. Finally, begin to pray for them. Ask the Holy Spirit to guard your heart from anger towards them. If you are angry, it will make it harder to do this process well. Praying for them helps to keep you from getting angry. If you don't get the resolution you want, keep kindly enforcing your boundaries regarding conduct in meetings and the like. Let your hard work and character be known.

The good news is that Christine saw God be faithful to His promises as she acted upon these principles with one of her colleagues. Her calm demeanor and candor elicited an immediate apology from her colleague and led to a better working relationship.

Conflict resolution is actually a sign of great strength. It takes maturity to look someone in the eye and calmly ask about the tensions or offenses without getting defensive. Most important to remember is that every conflict is an opportunity for God to be glorified. You don't know how much your humility will make an impact for the gospel.

7. Stay Off the Slippery Slope of Sexual Sin

Your job is a great opportunity to earn money and support yourself, to increase your skills, to do interesting tasks . . . and to become ensnared in sexual sin. In fact, eighty-five percent of extramarital affairs start in the workplace.[7]

As you start your career, you should assume you are just as vulnerable, and establish some practices now that will help you maintain wise, God-honoring boundaries. First, recognize that alcohol fuels many escapades that wouldn't have started in the sober light of day. I once knew a woman who had been on staff with a ministry and eventually transitioned to working for a large company. She was one of the few women in her office and one of the few single adults, as well. A business trip with too many drinks led to a disastrous sexual encounter with one of her married colleagues. In the light of day, she was horrified at what happened—it was totally out of character for her and ruined all the years of sexual purity she had maintained. Her bad decisions started with the excessive alcohol she consumed.

Because business travel presents an opportunity for temptation, think ahead about how you will avoid a story like my friend's above.

Psychologist Dave Carder says business travelers "are on a slippery slope headed for trouble" when wining and dining out of town: "Secrecy is the protection; alcohol is the barrier buster; and availability lights the fire."[8] Recognizing the hazards of late-night accessibility, one business executive says she is always in her hotel room by 10:00 p.m. when on business travel.[9]

Be cognizant of the fact that working together builds some level of intimacy. But friendship doesn't have to become detrimental if you guard your thought life—and the intimacies that you share or receive. Be warm and friendly, but be wary of the married coworker who wants to talk to you about his marital woes and is looking for comfort and support elsewhere. In all my years of working, I've never seen where that ever went anywhere good.

Finally, cultivate accountability partners and good friends outside of work who can help you sort through the inevitable attractions that will arise in the workplace. The secret crush loses a lot of its painful hold when examined by rational friends who aren't in its chokehold. We all have these crushes and attractions—but we can prevent disappointment, awkward speculation, or sinful results through making others privy to our thoughts and daydreams.

8. Invest in the Private Sphere

As you launch into adulthood, it's good to invest in your career. Assuming you are single and childless, you can spend more time and effort on the job than at home. But don't become a slave to your job. You are more than that. You belong to Christ and He values the investments you make in the private sphere as well.

Wherever you live, you are still a part of a household as defined by Scripture. You can still exercise dominion over your private sphere as a single woman. Consider that you shouldn't wait for marriage to learn basic household skills, like food preparation, laundry, and cleaning. There is nothing worse than waking up on the morning of a big meeting to find that you have run out of shampoo, or forgotten to pick up the dry cleaning, or left for the office on an empty stomach because you ran out of food. Good household management is a characteristic of a godly woman.

You are not just called to manage your home for your own benefit, but Scripture also requires you to use your home for the benefit of others (1 Tim. 5:10 specifically, and also Rom. 12:13; Heb. 13:2). No matter your living arrangement, you can still invest in the lives that are nourished there—show hospitality to roommates, friends, neighbors, church friends, or extended family.

These years are a prime time to learn how to invest in your values and priorities outside of work too. Rather than being driven by your schedule, consider how you are investing in your relationships, your church, and the Great Commission, then make sure your calendar reflects time for those values.

Consider, too, the investment you are making in your health and well-being and prioritize regular exercise, healthy sleep habits, and Sabbath rest. The habits you establish now will help you if you have a family in the future—because it becomes more of a balancing act when you have them.

As young women, remember that you have just launched into your career. The first choices you make won't be the last. A career is a journey, filled with decisions that you make in faith. You need to remember that it is not all up to you and that you don't need to have it all figured out. "A man's heart plans his way, but the LORD determines his steps" (Prov. 16:9). We are all still trying to figure out what we want to be when we grow up, but that's because ambitions aren't worth having unless you want to grow with them.

CHAPTER 11

The Balancing Act

I (Nora) was running late. There had been traffic all the way into the city to the catering event where I was headed. But by my clock, I still had about thirty minutes before the guests were supposed to arrive. Despite being late, all I had to do was reheat and lay everything out. I thought I could do it.

The event was at one of those homes in Washington, D.C., that are unassuming from the outside, but worth millions. The only problem was that it was split into three levels, and the refrigerator on the bottom level had everything in it that I needed. So, I did what any sensible caterer would do: I piled my arms full for the trek up two flights of stairs.

There was the shrimp appetizer tray on the bottom, followed by the stacks of smoked salmon and gourmet pasta. And on the top front edge, the square container of spaghetti sauce fit just right.

As I entered the foyer, I turned to close the door behind me. I can still feel the terrible sensation today. The pile in my arms shifted . . . and the spaghetti sauce slid off the stack.

Spaghetti sauce and white marble don't blend, just in case you were wondering. It went everywhere. The guests were about to arrive, so I quickly tried to clean it up. The clients probably found it later under doorjambs and on their potted plants, as well.

When you are balancing family and a career, it's messy. You stack all of it up, hoping something won't fall off and cause a royal disaster. Welcome to the season called the balancing act. As we enter into our thirties, our expectations have already experienced a few casualties. We expected to find a great job out of school, but may find ourselves stuck in entry-level work. We expected to find the right guy after a couple of relationships, but some of us end up on the dating circuit much longer.

Or we get married only to be divorced shortly thereafter. We expect to achieve financial stability, but many in the Millennial generation fared poorly with the abrupt change in the economy. Some of us even went backwards, like the 25 percent of us ages twenty to thirty-four who returned to live in our parents' homes (I'm twice guilty).[1]

Unexpected Grace

For Jessica, this time in her life started as a happy stay-at-home mother, rearing four children and enjoying domestic life. Then her husband abandoned the family, wiping them out financially. With no advance warning, Jessica was thrown into the breadwinner role.

"I grew up with the mentality that I was just going to get married and have kids," she says. "Growing up, my mom didn't work. I didn't know any moms who worked. I thought I would just be a mom and be busy at home. I never had a back-up plan because I thought I wouldn't need to do anything else. Honestly, looking back, I wish I had been more proactive in figuring out what I could do professionally."

Now Jessica supports herself and her family with a home-based graphic design business, which allows her to care for her children as a single parent. She says it's tough: "I have to be very diligent to be compartmentalized," she says. "I have time scheduled to answer e-mails, time scheduled to concept ideas, and time scheduled to be a mom. Obviously I am a mom all the time, but given our financial pressures I also could work all the time. So knowing when I am scheduled to work takes the pressure off of me during mom time. I know when I'm supposed to work so I can be present for my kids."

Through hard experiences, Jessica also discovered she held a false assumption: that grace made things easy. "I learned that grace doesn't always look the way that we expect it to. We need to be okay with that and not question whether it's really grace," she says. "The reality is that it's hard to be a working parent. I feel so maxed out and stretched in every way. But God has sustained and upheld me. He has given me stamina. Looking back, it's so obvious. But in the midst of it, it *felt* very hard."

By contrast, Shana grew up with the opposite experience. As a single African-American woman, she says that it never occurred to her to consider being a stay-at-home mom: "Culturally speaking, black women don't typically stay at home. They work. That was the example I saw as normal in my community. My mom and grandmother created very loving and happy families, but never made it an imperative that my sister, cousins, and I get married and have children. For my family, it was more important that we grow up, get a job, provide for ourselves, and not face discrimination. We were trained to seek success outside of the home."

Growing up, Shana felt the women in her church looked down on her family because both of her parents worked while she and her sister were babysat. "In my family we loved each other very much and I had fantastic parents who never missed a beat in terms of providing for us and being there for us," she recalls. "But we infrequently ate dinner together, we didn't do family devotions, and we went to public school. I really enjoyed my childhood, but I got the impression at church that perhaps my family was somehow 'not right' because we did or didn't do certain things. I felt a bit judged."

Now as an adult, she's asking questions about how to balance the biblical emphasis on homemaking within her cultural norms of professional and familial success.

"There's not really a model of a 'stay-at-home-1950s-housewife' in black culture (even Claire Huxtable on *The Cosby Show* worked), so it was generally assumed that the housewife model was a white people thing," she says. "Even getting to a suitable marriage can be a challenge. Marrying well is made more difficult because there is a shortage of available Christian African-American men due to dearth of solid churches in the African-American community and numerous broken families. Should you desire to marry within the culture, it's very difficult to find a match.

"But despite the demographical odds and cultural norms, I'm beginning to see that making your home this awesome center of productivity and practicing hospitality (which I do now as a single female), and loving your husband and children transcends both the black views of family and white views of family."

Both in their early thirties, Jessica and Shana have already seen how hard it is when your expectations and cultural norms about productivity collide with reality. Their experiences may speak to you too. You may be single like Shana and reading this chapter might be hard for you.

You may be wondering if you will have a family and what that will look like. Or you may be wondering how this syncs with your culture and upbringing. Don't skip this chapter because you think it may not apply to you. It does. Or like Jessica, you may be a busy mother who only can read a few pages each day. In either case, this chapter is not about either/ or choices. We're not adding to the "Mommy Wars." You can lower your guard. We are looking for unexpected grace.

This is the time to discard all the one-size-fits-all ideas you may have, so that you can open your eyes to the unique way the Lord has equipped you to balance your productivity with other responsibilities He has given you. By looking to Jesus, and walking with Him, we can be confident that "those who look to him are radiant, and their faces shall never be ashamed" (Ps. 34:5 ESV).

Tough Choices

A lot of times we can feel guilty about the choices we make. Jessica regrets that she did not plan for a career when she was younger. Shana regrets developing such an identity in her career that it made her downplay the importance of productivity in the home. I (Nora) have felt pulled to make choices in both directions, toward career and towards family life.

Sometimes I've had to work because we desperately needed the money, other times I chose to work, and now I'm choosing to be at home. The first time I left my eight-week-old daughter with her grandmother to speak at a conference, I was thrilled to get out and do something different than breastfeeding. But as a working mother, I felt that anxious pressure every single time I was running late to work and every single moment as I raced back to my kids.

On the flipside, there are days when it is so hard to train little children, that I want to quit full-time motherhood and go back to work. The thought of being able to eat an uninterrupted lunch entices me to the Internet for job postings.

This is when we have to turn to God and ask Him for faith. Our response to the work in front of us needs to be based on faith, not our churning emotions, or the opinions of others. We need to make decisions about work and family wisely, and with counsel, but we also must have a sense of faith for those decisions.

When I moved from Arizona to Washington, D.C., for Travis's new job, I was so busy with the move that by the time I slowed down, the transition to full-time motherhood caught me by surprise. In my excitement, I didn't realize that I had left everything I knew about myself behind in Arizona. I suddenly felt uncertain about who I was. For the first time, I was staying at home in a new place without the social network I had built. I loved the extra time with my children, but still found myself at a loss as to how to shape my new status—or lack thereof.

Turning to my Bible, I was comforted by this Scripture:

> But someone will ask, "How are the dead raised?
> With what kind of body do they come?" You foolish
> person! What you sow does not come to life unless it
> dies. And what you sow is not the body that is to be,
> but a bare kernel, perhaps of wheat or of some other
> grain. But God gives it a body as he has chosen, and
> to each kind of seed its own body. For not all flesh is
> the same, but there is one kind for humans, another
> for animals, another for birds, and another for fish.
> There are heavenly bodies and earthly bodies, but the
> glory of the heavenly is of one kind, and the glory of
> the earthly is of another. There is one glory of the sun,
> and another glory of the moon, and another glory
> of the stars; for star differs from star in glory. So is
> it with the resurrection of the dead. What is sown is
> perishable; what is raised is imperishable. It is sown in
> dishonor; it is raised in glory. It is sown in weakness;
> it is raised in power. (1 Cor. 15:35–43 ESV)

This passage about the promise of the resurrection whispered to me: Was I ready to let go of who I used to be? Was I ready to let go of what I expected? Was I ready to be nothing but a seed again?

I had to embrace the adjustments of my new reality. I had to be willing to let my identity go. I wasn't Nora, the active Arizona mom. I wasn't Nora, the dietitian. I was just Nora, the woman God had made.

I wasn't lost. God knew me—He knew exactly who He made me to be and what decisions He was leading me to make.

Transitions are bumpy, even the happy ones. We all go through them at some point. It takes time to adjust. Often, we feel like we should be much farther ahead than we are—unless we remember that "bare kernels" are always sown in weakness. It's not bad to have your identity change. God promises that if we trust Him, He will replant us to reap eternal rewards.

Numbered Days

But here's the surprising reality: according to one recent survey, 84 percent of mothers said that staying home to raise their children is a financial luxury to which they aspire. What's more, more than one in three women resent their partner for not earning enough to make that dream a reality.[2] When I (Nora) read that statistic, it surprised me because recent statistics show that 70 percent of American women with children under eighteen are employed.[3] Not to mention the 9.9 million single mothers who have children under eighteen and must work.[4]

The conflict between the stay-at-home mom camp and the working-mom camp is heated. Each side thinks the problem is about a choice; but neither has identified the real problem.

The Bible clearly says that fruitfulness in a fallen world is hard. It says that childbearing will be hard for women (Gen. 3:16). It's not the difficulty of the labor pains; it's the burden of carrying on our work outside of Eden. If we don't acknowledge the broken system, and it's only solution, redemption, we'll always be trying to find a solution that is "good enough."

Author Tim Challies says, "For the foundation of the moral significance of our work is not what our work is, but whether or not we are doing it in faith and to God's glory (Eph. 6:5–9)."[5] The Reformation fought to restore the biblical idea that all kinds of work have value, and that spiritual work isn't more valuable to God than secular work. If we put a stake in the ground that all lawful and edifying work matters to God, then we can go and ask God for wisdom to make good decisions.

Not being a parent, I (Carolyn) can duck the volleys of guilt served up in the "Mommy Wars." What I do have to offer is the perspective of time, having watched both sides expend a lot of effort over the years telling women exactly how to live their lives to one set pattern. But time eventually showed the limitations of this one-size-fits-all advice.

Time itself is the benchmark for wisdom. Psalm 90:12 says, "Teach us to number our days carefully so that we may develop wisdom in our hearts." The result of developing a heart of wisdom is found in the closing lines of this psalm: "Let the favor of the Lord our God be on us; establish for us the work of our hands—establish the work of our hands" (v. 17).

Numbering our days means we recognize that we have time limitations. We can't cram more hours in between the rising of the sun and the setting of the sun, nor can we go back in time. We can't rewind the lives of children. We can't rewind our marriages to find more time together. Looking back makes it easy to evaluate our choices, but God is asking us to develop that perspective now.

The idea that we can do two incredibly demanding, full-time tasks at the same time is a false illusion. When we multitask, we might believe we can do two things at the same time, but brain research shows we actually just mentally toggle back and forth between the tasks, losing time in the trade-off.[6]

There are reams and reams and *reams* of articles about couples who are stressed out trying to juggle childrearing and full-time jobs. No matter how they try to negotiate the workload, there's simply too much of it to go round. You can't equally divide what is too much for two people to do and still expect it all will get done. So perhaps the best way to look at this balancing act is to question its very existence.

Author Andi Ashworth says we have normalized frantic lifestyles when we don't need to do so. Women in our generation just aren't good at slowing down.[7] A recent article said the frenzy to try to do it all results only in burnout by age thirty for young women, and a realization that they haven't made time for relationships.[8]

If we "number our days carefully," then we have to evaluate the time we are given. We need wisdom to evaluate our long-term priorities, and consider what we can do at the present time. Sometimes, this means making difficult decisions, like scaling down to one income so a parent can be home with young children; for others, it means going back to work for a season or longer.

My friends, Jared and Liz, pursued an entrepreneurial solution. Jared built a business as a sound editor for games, film, and television and as he expanded, he added his wife, Liz, as the client contact, handling scheduling, e-mails, and deadline panics. When their first child was on the way, Jared crunched the numbers and they decided it was far more cost-effective for Liz to keep working from home and pay for cleaning and other household help, rather than to replace her in the business. But when their child arrived, they found it was more challenging to care for a baby than they anticipated. For now, Liz is happy being a full-time, stay-at-home mother, while Jared is back to client management. They say that their decision may change in the future, but at present this is best for both their business *and* family.

Applying business principles like scheduling, time-management, and outsourcing are key for prioritizing the important relationships at home. The woman who "numbers her days carefully" has to persist in applying wisdom to her time, despite the pressures around her to conform to a certain standard of "success" in the home and as a parent.

The Little People

In her book, *Real Love for Real Life: The Art and Work of Caring*, Andi Ashworth paints a compelling picture of the blessings and benefits that come from investing in other people. Her portrait of the creativity and community that arise from investing in the private sphere is exceedingly attractive. Even with this high view of family and the home, she offers this perspective to help us think through the competing priorities of family and work:

> The assumption is often made that mothers should do the lion's share of the child rearing, and yet this idea is completely contrary to Scripture. The Bible gives us a clear picture of intimate, long-term care from both parents. The Old Testament is filled with instructions to both parents to teach their children God's Word and God's ways. (Deuteronomy 4:9; 11:19 and Proverbs 1:8; 6:20 offer some examples of this.) Ephesians 6:4 commands fathers to bring up their children "in

the training and instruction of the Lord." The verb
translated "bring up" has to do first with bodily nour-
ishment and then with education in its entirety.

Not only is the scriptural mandate for both fathers
and mothers to teach, train, instruct and nurture their
children, but in a broad overview of Scripture, we find
both men and women doing a *mixture* of economic
and caring work. . . . Both sexes are called to practice
hospitality, to care intimately for children, to provide for
extended family, and to love and serve the body of Christ
as well as the wider world in real, life-supporting ways.[9]

For most of us in our childbearing years, our investment will be in
very little people. While we recognize that not every woman can and
will stay home with her children during their entire childhoods, we will
point out that Scripture has a very high view of parenting. If God gives
you children, the training and nurturing of these children can't be done
in the leftovers of a busy day.

Parenting is an intense vocation of its own. God has given you the
responsibility of training your children to the best of your ability and
those days are numbered. If you have the U.S. average of 2.6 children,
each about three years apart, the initial commitment of full-time,
intense parenting will last about fifteen years just to get them to kindergarten. Now, parenting is never "over" and older children also require
times of intense training and focus, but we understand that the work is
hard and can feel never-ending.

My (Carolyn's) sister says that as a full-time mother she misses her
annual review. Whenever she got her review on the job, she knew exactly
how well she was doing against her performance goals. But mothering
can be a long stretch of unappreciated labor.

Two encouragements for moms who might be reading this: first, the
work you are doing has eternal significance so don't give up. If you are
raising your children to fear the Lord, then you have already given them
an incredible inheritance.

Second, remember that your sacrifices will be rewarded: "So don't
throw away your confidence, which has a great reward. *For you need
endurance,* so that after you have done God's will, you may receive what
was promised" (Heb. 10:35–36, emphasis added).

Off-Ramping and On-Ramping

The world we live in doesn't make the balancing act any easier. As we saw in the modern history chapter, even though women have been participating in the workforce in greater numbers over the last century, our nation's laws and culture are not generally favorable to working mothers. According to the annual State of the World's Mothers Report from the Save the Children Foundation, the U.S. has one of the least generous maternity leave policies of any wealthy nation: "It is the only developed country—and one of only a handful of countries world-wide—that does not guarantee paid leave for working moms."[10]

According to a recent White House report, women now make up 50 percent of the American workforce.[11] Yet many workplace policies still make it hard for women to "on-ramp" and "off-ramp" their careers as needed. A post-Recession study showed that 73 percent of women trying to return to the workforce after a voluntary timeout for childcare or other reasons have trouble finding a job. Those who do return lose 16 percent of their earning power, over 25 percent report a decrease in management responsibilities, and 22 percent had to step down to a lower job title. But a full 69 percent of women say that they wouldn't have off-ramped if their companies had offered flexible work options such as reduced-hour schedules, job sharing, part-time career tracks or short unpaid sabbaticals.[12]

The question that remains then, is how much more could the economy grow if the full potential of women now sidelined or underused is unleashed through flexible work schedules? It's a win for *families*, not just "women."

That's why it takes creative planning. If you do plan on having children, you will need to consider how "off-ramping" your career will affect your marketability. Don't just assume it will kill your career. In teaching or health-related fields, you are only required to keep up on your certifications and continuing education. For others, it will require creativity to keep your skills fresh and up-to-speed. Think outside the box: paid work isn't the only thing that can fill in a gap on a résumé. Think about the story you'll tell a future employer about how the time you've used to do other things has made you a better worker.

But even with all the best planning, you may find you have a similar reaction to Mary Matalin. In the book *Midlife Crisis at 30*, Matalin recalls when the stress of her White House job provided sudden clarity: "I finally asked myself, 'Who needs me more?' And that's when I realized, it's somebody else's turn to do this job. I'm indispensable to my kids, but I'm not close to indispensable to the White House." She goes on to add:

> If you want to know the solution, this is it: Having
> control over your schedule is the only way that women
> who want to have a career and a family can make it
> work. You've got to look for ways to create options for
> yourself that don't necessarily fall on a linear career
> path. All that stuff about goal setting and career tra-
> jectories is oversold and distracting.
>
> My absolute favorite statistic is the phenomenal
> rate of growth of women-owned businesses—the
> entrepreneurial path is emerging as the practical solu-
> tion to the impossible juggling act.[13]

I (Carolyn) agree with Matalin—to a point. Being an entrepreneur is extremely time-consuming and requires everything you have and then some to get it off the ground. I jokingly say that now I work for the craziest boss ever: myself. In the early years of my business, I have averaged more than sixty-hour workweeks. I can't imagine having done that with a family.

As an on-call dietitian, I (Nora) agree with Matalin about the perks of scheduling. I could pick the days at the hospitals where I wanted to work, as well as pick the hours I saw clients in a private practice. But from my experience of owning a catering business, I know I am better off supporting someone else's small business rather than go at it alone, which is why I joined up with another dietitian in her established practice.

Beyond entrepreneurial solutions, there are other glimmers of hope for working mothers. Job-sharing, flexible work schedules, telecommuting, and unpaid leave policies have been adopted by many companies nationwide. A recent survey of companies shows that between 2005 and

2012, more employers are now offering at least twelve weeks of leave for women following childbirth.

We have to remain flexible as the dynamics of the workplace, and our lives, change. "Off-ramping" and "on-ramping" may happen multiple times in our lives. We need to be prepared that success is never a direct route; it often has many twists and turns.

To Think Better

More important than changes in our social system or the law, or even creative planning, we need to agree as Christians to think differently about productivity. Kate Harris, a mother and executive director with the Washington Institute, a Christian nonprofit organization focused on vocation, writes perceptively about this experience:

> "Work" is a term that tends to lose its meaning in discussions about motherhood because of its narrow application as a synonym for career-oriented occupations. As Christians, our definition of work is infinitely more inclusive than that. . . . [A]s mothers seek better understanding of their work and identity, it is important to keep in mind the practical context that governs how they live into their day-to-day responsibilities. The comprehensive realities of life, such as whether a husband works from home or travels frequently, whether family is nearby or far away, if finances allow room for extra help or require extra income, if kids are healthy or not healthy, if marriage is stable and happy or requires extra effort—these are all enormously consequential in how we come to steward our responsibilities faithfully. Not all work is for all seasons, and at the same time, some work is perennial and will inevitably find ways to sprout up. In every instance we need to carefully discern what work we are to pursue—or not pursue—in light of our other responsibilities.

In all of this, whether it be language, category
or context, it is essential for mothers to recognize
that the goal in exploring identity in light of work is
not to do more or be busier, but rather *to think better*
about the ways we engage the fullness of our callings.
For some women, it will mean granting themselves
permission to explore interests, skills or opportunities that persist outside, alongside or amidst their
responsibilities as a mom. For others it means evaluating whether or not their priorities and commitments
are properly aligned with the commitments they
have to their family. For all women, it means being
humble enough to step outside the bounds of our own
comfort and offer the fullness of our gifts in service to
Christ, trusting that if it's His work to do He will provide the margin needed to do it.[14] (emphasis added)

The Bible says, "those who promote peace have joy" (Prov. 12:20).
The ESV version says those who "plan peace have joy." As Christians, we
know that no plan guarantees our joy, but there is something to be said
for making plans that promote the maximum amount of peace and joy
in your life. Over-assumptions of your capacity will only leave you har-
ried, anxious, and unable to handle the inevitable "expected volatility"
of a full life. The future is never what we assume, but it's never a waste
of time to anticipate options and plan for certain contingencies.

My friend Anne is thirty-five and seriously dating a man who has
two school-age children. They are talking about marriage and trying
to roadmap their future options. Anne has extensive experience in the
White House and State Department. She has the option to pursue a
lucrative public policy position, which would make hers the larger salary should they get married. She's not yet engaged, but she's trying to
make wise choices now by exploring the outcomes of her present choices
against possible futures. So she is measuring her job opportunities
against the possibility of getting married. She has asked her boyfriend to
imagine a typical day where she comes home later than he does. Would
he be okay with tending to his children after school and making dinner? What would family life look like? What would his expectations be?
What would hers be? Where might they have conflict? What if she gets

pregnant and she wants to stay home with their children? How would they afford that? And so on. They are actually taking a premarital counseling course even before getting engaged just to make sure that they are considering the experiences and perspectives of others.

This couple is asking really great questions, ones that we have to ask ourselves. They have wisely seen that if you try to carry too much, something is going to slide off and hit the floor hard—just like spaghetti sauce on a white marble floor, it will be a difficult mess to clean up.

Despite the limitations of our plans, and the mistakes we might make, we have a greater resource in God. He gives us wisdom to evaluate our plans: "The counsel of the LORD stands forever, the plans of His heart from generation to generation" (Ps. 33:11). He thinks more long term than we do and His heart is *for* us: not just for us as parents, but for the next generation.

CHAPTER 12

Coaching for Success

By midlife, most women are managing sprawling enterprises. Whether the Lord's providence has led you to a full-time homemaking position, a full-time career, or a mix of both, chances are you have multiple direct reports—be they teens at home or staff members at work—and complicated logistics that keep you on the run.

This season of life is about helping others achieve success. Your job as a midlife manager, mother, or wife can be described as coaching others to greatness. At home or at work, you are building a team—and the required skill sets are extraordinarily similar. (If you don't yet have a team to coach, keep on reading so you are prepared in advance for this responsibility.)

I am glad I became an employer before I had the opportunity to write this book. The company I lead is very small, but the perspective shift I experienced was profound. Now that I'm in charge of the big picture, I realize how many factors are involved in day-to-day operations. Management is more challenging than I perceived. I also realize that when I was an employee, I had a vastly inflated opinion of my performance. My current colleagues are actually way better at accepting my direction than I ever was with my own supervisors. Looking back, I am convinced that some of the actions I perceived as an employee to be micro-management were actually an attempt to make me accountable for my time and progress.

No matter whether you have arrived at this chapter wondering if women should manage men, or if you have turned here seeking advice on cultivating executive presence, in this chapter we are going to examine what makes a woman a good coach as a manager or business leader.

"Only a Woman"

The course of human history reveals that men have consistently underrated what women can do and achieve. When Elizabeth I was crowned Queen of England in 1558, she had already survived numerous political intrigues and revolts. Her reign provided relative stability and peace to England during her forty-four years on the throne and the arts flourished during this time. Yet she had to consistently overcome the low expectations of her womanliness. Her reign raised England's status abroad, especially after the tremendous defeat of the Spanish Armada. Yet Pope Sixtus V said of her: "She is only a woman, only mistress of half an island, and yet she makes herself feared by Spain, by France, by the Empire, by all."[1]

The question through the ages has been: "Can a woman manage?" This distortion of women's capabilities is not found in a biblical perspective. There is no biblical prohibition against women directing the labor of men. As theologian Wayne Grudem writes, "What we find in the Bible is that God has given commands that establish male leadership in the *home* and in the *church*, but that other teachings in His Word give considerable freedom in other areas of life. We should not try to require either more or less than Scripture itself requires."[2]

That said, we are made female in the image of God, and there's something wonderfully distinctive about being a woman. We don't have to mimic masculinity to manage well. In fact, mimicry will typically backfire as it is forced and unnecessary. It also overlooks the wonderful qualities that women possess and diminishes what the Lord has created in us. The warm, gracious, and encouraging confidence of a woman can go a long way to building a good team.

My favorite portrait of feminine management and initiative is found in Abigail's story in the Old Testament. In 1 Samuel 25, we learn that Abigail is married to a wealthy but foolish man named Nabal. The Bible describes him as a very rich man who was shearing his sheep— the equivalent of harvest time. In other words, it was payday. David sends a request to share in the feast day because his men helped Nabal's shepherds guard his extensive flocks in the wilderness. Nabal foolishly dismisses the request and provokes David to a murderous rage.

So one of Nabal's servants rushes to Abigail, an industrious woman who has already overseen the preparations for the feast of "200 loaves of bread, two skins of wine, five butchered sheep, a bushel of roasted grain, 100 clusters of raisins, and 200 cakes of pressed figs" (v. 18) and he implores her to "consider carefully" what she should do. He is counting on her to forestall impending disaster for the family business. So she loads these provisions on donkeys and sends them ahead to David and his men.

Abigail is described as "intelligent and beautiful" in verse 3 but her husband was described as "harsh and evil in his dealings." As we will see, this account praises Abigail for her wisdom and initiative, but says nothing beyond the fact that she was beautiful. She does not trade on her physical charms, though no doubt they were evident to all, especially David. When she encounters him, she does not use false feminine flattery or emotional manipulation to sway his purpose. She does not flirt, she does not cry. What she does is confront David to warn him of the consequences of his actions and to urge him to live up to God's standards:

> Please forgive your servant's offense, for the LORD is
> certain to make a lasting dynasty for my lord because
> he fights the LORD's battles. Throughout your life,
> may evil not be found in you. When someone pursues
> you and attempts to take your life, my lord's life will
> be tucked safely in the place where the LORD your
> God protects the living. However, He will fling away
> your enemies' lives like stones from a sling. When
> the LORD does for my lord all the good He promised
> and appoints you ruler over Israel, there will not be
> remorse or a troubled conscience for my lord because
> of needless bloodshed or my lord's revenge. And
> when the LORD does good things for my lord, may
> you remember me your servant." Then David said to
> Abigail, "Praise to the LORD God of Israel, who sent
> you to meet me today! Your discernment is blessed,
> and you are blessed. Today you kept me from partici-
> pating in bloodshed and avenging myself by my own
> hand." (1 Sam. 25:28–33)

This was a woman who used all of her resources, wisdom, initiative, and bold words to call a man to emulate a higher standard—and trusted the Lord for the outcome. Abigail managed this situation shrewdly and did so to protect the lives of her servants who would have been attacked by David's army. She was bold, effective, and strategic in protecting the assets and employees of her family's business. And *thoroughly feminine*. We see in the Bible that these qualities are not contradictory.

Coaching or Cliques

When you think of coaching others to success, perhaps the picture that popped up in your mind was that of the red-faced coach screaming epithets and threats from the sidelines to his team, a stream of vulgarity and discouragement that is supposed to elicit greatness out of the players.

That is not the picture of a good coach. So perhaps I ought to have used the concept of a cheerleader, instead? No, the women who stand on the sidelines trading on their sexuality, offering general encouragement without any direct or strategic impact on the team is not what I picture either.

Both of these images are a distortion. Godly masculinity is not abusive. Godly femininity is not sexually provocative. A good coach of either gender is supposed to call forth the best possible qualities and performances of his or her team by providing the resources, tools, and guidance needed to achieve concrete and specific goals. Management is really a form of serving—meaning it is directed at making others the best they can be in order to achieve a larger goal.

This concept is clearly presented in a recent study published in the *Harvard Business Review*. It shows that when women do reach higher levels of management, they actually outscore their male counterparts in a number of management leadership qualities:

> Most stereotypes would have us believe that female
> leaders excel at "nurturing" competencies such as
> developing others and building relationships, and
> many might put exhibiting integrity and engaging
> in self-development in that category as well. And in

all four cases our data concurred—women did score
higher than men. But the women's advantages were
not at all confined to traditionally women's strengths.
In fact at every level, more women were rated by their
peers, their bosses, their direct reports, and their other
associates as better overall leaders than their male
counterparts—and the higher the level, the wider that
gap grows. . . .

Specifically, at all levels, women are rated higher
in fully 12 of the 16 competencies that go into
outstanding leadership. And two of the traits where
women outscored men to the highest degree—taking initiative and driving for results—have long been
thought of as particularly male strengths. As it happened, men outscored women significantly on only
one management competence in this survey—the
ability to develop a strategic perspective.[3]

What are the leadership competencies in this study? They are the
qualities of truly great coaches:

- Takes Initiative
- Practices Self-Development
- Displays High Integrity and Honesty
- Drives for Results
- Develops Others
- Inspires and Motivates Others
- Builds Relationships
- Collaboration and Teamwork
- Establishes Stretch Goals
- Champions Change
- Solves Problems and Analyzes Issues
- Communicates Powerfully and Prolifically
- Connects the Group to the Outside World
- Innovates
- Technical or Professional Expertise
- Develops Strategic Perspective

Notice how many of these competencies revolve around communication and relationship development—inspiring, motivating, building, connecting, and developing the team. Whether or not we are managers, women can be fantastic coaches if we use our words to build others up. When we don't, we create the dynamic Paul addressed in 1 Timothy 5:13, regarding young widows who were idle: "They are not only idle, but are also gossips and busybodies, saying things they shouldn't say."

One of the comments I received in an informal survey I conducted about women managers was about this communication hurdle: "One of the biggest problems I deal with is the gossip that goes around. I work with primarily girls, so it is common. People starting and spreading rumors. I wish there were more communication between people, because so much would be better if there were set expectations and honesty."

While it's true that "who you know" can be as important as "what you know" on the job, there is a relational power play that often happens in the workplace between women. It is the kind of game teen girls specialize in—the public ostracization or acceptance of individuals—that should be out of bounds, especially for adult women. But this doesn't just happen in the office; it can exist on the sidelines of a soccer game, at PTA meetings, or, sadly, in church.

When it happens, you have to clearly refuse to play those games. I once had a vendor tell me that she didn't want me working with another vendor because that woman was manipulative and selfish. She kept trying to enforce this demand, but I noticed that the other woman—the one who was labeled so harshly—was nothing except professional and supportive. I had to go back to the gossiping vendor and clearly explain that while I had heard her cautions, at this point I had no basis for coming to the same conclusion and therefore I would treat them both equally. I would not be emotionally manipulated into taking sides in a conflict that I had nothing to do with and preceded my involvement.

Good coaches keep the team focused on objective goals, insist that personal conflicts be worked out or kept off the field, and build up team members through skills development and timely praise rather than threats and anger. Coaches exist to develop a team that operates better together than as a collection of individuals.

Put Your Pads On

Coaches know that they are sending their players onto a rough field. Their players are going to take a pounding from the opposite team. So good coaches make sure that their team members are appropriately suited up with the protective padding they need to play. Padding keeps you safe when you take a hard hit. But your players may have no idea that they need to gear up for taking a hit. And sometimes coaches can forget this principle too.

Years ago I had a job where God used my colleagues to show me the extent of my defensiveness and pride. I was called out all the time and it was uncomfortable. I think I spent at least half of my first year fighting tears of frustration, stress, and anger. Sometimes I kept them under check and sometimes they checked me. I am not pretty when I tear up. There's nothing delicate and feminine about my red nose and eyes, not to mention the swollen eyelids the next day that make me look reptilian. As hard as I tried to get vanity to rein in my emotions, there were times when the blasted tears won.

It can be a hard thing to learn but work is not personal. It's not a perpetual blind date, where you are trying to figure out if you are liked and approved. You were hired to do a task and it's your ability to this task that is being evaluated. As female managers, we can help younger women "put their pads on" by teaching them not to confuse the evaluation of their work performance with any sense of approval as a person.

Author Shaunti Feldhahn offers some good insights here. She surveyed numerous men, asking if there was anything they have seen talented women do that undermines their effectiveness with men, simply because the women don't realize how it is perceived. The most common answer she heard was, "Women sometimes take things too personally." One executive explained it this way: "When we tell employees they need to improve, the men just hear, 'You did not do what we needed. What will you do to get better?' When we work with the women, we can have the same data in front of us, but they seem to hear, *We do not like you.*"[4]

One woman told me that she has learned not to respond when strong emotions are present—either good or bad. She waits twenty-four hours to properly process her reactions and respond. If your workflow allows for that time to pause, I think this is a wise idea. As Feldhahn writes, strong emotions are perceived differently at work when they come from women:

> As one man put it, "The moment I see someone tearing up, I think, 'There goes the logical part of this conversation. We can now abandon logic.' Men think if someone is crying they've ceased to be logical."
>
> While a particularly intense flood of emotion makes it difficult for anyone to think clearly, science shows that women's emotional threshold is, in essence, much higher than men's. Women can experience strong feelings and still be able to think clearly, but because men usually can't, they think women can't either. To men, emotion is irrational in many ways.[5]

There are also other things we can do to help manage our emotions. Adequate sleep, rest, exercise, and healthy diets help to minimize the negative effects our bodies have on our emotions. The same goes for hormones.

Let me assure you that huge hormonal swings don't have to be endured as "normal." I was hormonally out-of-whack for most of my twenties and didn't know how to treat it. My personal conviction is that it's better to find a doctor who will treat what is off-balance and not just mask your symptoms with more medications. But as you seek medical treatment, remember that above and beyond medical treatment, we have a great Physician. He gives grace that is sufficient even for your hormones. When I would feel that *trapped-animal-trying-to-gnaw-its-way-out-of-my-skin* sensation of PMS, I knew it was time to turn to Jesus and ask for a "double portion" of His sweet spirit to help me respond gently to whatever was coming my way that day.

For many years, the verse that was taped to my computer was from Philippians 4:5: "Let your gentleness be evident to all. The Lord is near." That's the NIV translation. The ESV translates it as "reasonableness" and the HCSB translates it as "graciousness." I think it takes all three words to give us the fullness of that idea—let your gentleness, reasonableness, and graciousness be known to all. Be gentle in your words. Be reasonable in your responses. Be gracious in your reactions to others.

You don't have to live in bondage to your hormones. It's possible to subdue them by the power of the Holy Spirit.

As managers, we have to help our team sort out their emotions and conflicts to ensure ongoing productivity. In some cases, it means having private conversations with individuals to understand the problems at hand. In other cases, it means calling together the warring factions for a conversation that you observe but don't mediate. You might have to be the jury and judge—especially if the conflict is about a violation of a clear company policy—but most often your job as a coach will be to see that the team gears up properly and learns to hash out offenses between themselves.

Clear Calls

It used to be that the most tedious part of transcribing the interviews we filmed was fast-forwarding through my long-winded questions to subjects, wherein I mused on a variety of thoughts and then stopped, expecting them to comment. Inevitably, they would ask, "Umm . . . so what is your question?"

Too many words. *FAIL.*

Top coaches have to master clear, concise communication. They can't afford a garbled call about the next play that confuses the team.

In the flood of e-mails, instant messages, and social media pings that everyone receives, we need to model brevity and clarity for those we manage. They need to have concrete tasks, goals, and outcomes. They also need to know we hired them to get the work done and that we are there to help them succeed.

My friend Lauren has been an executive at international media companies for many years. She sets clear expectations for her team at the hiring and review stages, and also defines how she wants them to work: "I let members of my team know that I recognize and value their taking initiative," she says. "Someone interested in advancement and leadership roles needs to be demonstrating clear thought processes, problem solving, and initiative. It's completely appropriate to use my feedback as a way to bounce ideas off of someone and as a check-in to ensure they are on the right path. But I want them to think about solutions to a challenge before they come to me."

Earlier in her career, she struggled with wanting to be seen as nice—not difficult or threatening—but learned that this can be a blind spot as a manager. "When I shifted from wanting to be liked to preferring to be respected, it allowed me to think about decisions in a different light. I think about what is right versus what may be popular, and how to say it without passive wording or confusing messages. It took some practice to give feedback based on facts and examples, without being emotional or girly/cute/sweet. There is a way to be decent and empathetic, yet direct and clear. It takes some work. But it has been a very useful style in my opinion."

As a single mother, she is especially sensitive to family issues on her team. "Until someone has had children, those who work with you in the office think you are not as invested if you have to leave early to get your children," she says. "But I find most moms that I have worked with are very efficient—they know how to use their time. They are usually the ones you can count on to get it done, get it done well, and get it done on time, because they want to get home and be with their families. They are motivated because they want to keep their jobs."

When Lauren first returned from maternity leave after having her son, her boss gave her a promotion and told her, "I don't expect you to work harder, I expect you to work smarter." Part of the working smarter was making sure others on the team and her boss had brief updates about what she was doing outside of the office. She worked in an international group at the time, so she would tell her boss what she did before she got to the office—like the 5:30 a.m. calls to Europe.

Now she pays that forward by helping other working parents on her team to be smart about their work-life juggles. One time one of her reports came to work on a public school holiday. So Lauren asked where this woman's eight-year-old child was and it turned out he was at home, alone. Lauren told her colleague to pack up her computer, head home to be with her child, and figure out a work-from-home schedule. This woman was afraid to ask for that schedule before Lauren ensured her it was okay. "I had to tell her, I promise you, if you continue to do your job, it will not negatively impact you at all," she says.

As much as clear communication helps direct reports know what to do, it is equally important for cultivating the "executive presence" that leads to C-suite positions. Interestingly, this description from a post on the *Harvard Business Review* blog shows how women can cultivate that executive presence without becoming shrill or aggressive:

> If you entered a room filled with twenty managers,
> Lydia Taylor, a member of the legal department,
> wouldn't stand out—but that would change once
> the dialogue started. Although soft spoken and not
> terribly aggressive, she was highly respected by her
> peers as well as the executives with whom she worked.
> Lydia possessed outstanding listening skills and had
> an unerring sense of when to enter the conversation
> to make her point. Unrushed, straightforward, and
> unflappable, she maintained her calm, even demeanor
> when others got emotional, and she used her dry
> sense of humor to defuse difficult situations. When
> challenged by others, she stood her ground in a firm,
> non-confrontational way. Although highly supportive
> of her internal customers, she was prepared to put her
> foot down if anyone advocated a position that might
> put the company at risk. As a result, Lydia was identi-
> fied as a top candidate and groomed to succeed the
> company's General Counsel.[6]

Expressing yourself is only one part of clear communication. This also depends on your ability to listen well. James 1:19–20 says, "Everyone must be quick to hear, slow to speak, and slow to anger, for man's anger does not accomplish God's righteousness." Proverbs says, "A wise man will listen and increase his learning" (1:5) and "The mind of the righteous person thinks before answering" (15:28).

The Bible reminds us that successful communication depends upon acquiring wisdom in our hearts, not just training our mouths. A heart that leans toward humility will inevitably lean toward constructive, clear, and loving language. Our speech should be an evidence of our faith. Words that are direct or empathetic will be much better received if they come from a woman with integrity in her Christian character. Speech that is precise, wise, and congruent to your character will not only be received better, it will motivate those you direct because they will see how well you model it.

The Head Coach Defines Success

Every winning team needs a great coach. But we need to realize that we are actually *assistant* coaches. We have a head coach in heaven who sees the entire team's contributions perfectly, who knows the motivations of all involved, and who is calling the shots to achieve success the way He defines it. The head coach knows how to create true champions and He has given us the playbook to memorize so we can perceive His calls and know His coaching philosophy:

> My son, do not forget my teaching, but let your heart
> keep my commandments, for length of days and
> years of life and peace they will add to you. Let not
> steadfast love and faithfulness forsake you; bind them
> around your neck; write them on the tablet of your
> heart. *So you will find favor and good success in the
> sight of God and man.* Trust in the LORD with all your
> heart, and do not lean on your own understanding.
> In all your ways acknowledge him, and he will make
> straight your paths. Be not wise in your own eyes; fear
> the Lord, and turn away from evil. (Prov. 3:1–7 ESV,
> emphasis added)

Verse four is the result of remembering and living godly principles: "So you will find favor and good success in the sight of God and man." As Christians, we shouldn't be looking to achieve a certain level of success just to impress others or win lots of awards; instead we should be asking and praying for the kind of success that draws people to the steadfast love of God. This is the head coach's ultimate mission and He defines a successful team by this benchmark.

A good illustration of this principle is found in the book of Genesis. Abraham's servant, who operated like his chief of staff, was sent on a mission to find a wife for Isaac, Abraham's son. As he went forward with this mission, he prayed, "LORD, God of my master Abraham, give me success today, and show kindness to my master Abraham" (Gen. 24:12). Then the servant asked the Lord to reveal His choice through the actions of a hospitable and hard-working woman who was willing to go above and beyond his own request for water by offering to draw extra water for his thirsty camels. He silently watched her work, waiting to see "whether or not the LORD had made his journey a success" (v. 21). When he discovered that the Lord had sent him to Abraham's clan, he rejoiced in the Lord's kindness.

There is no way to touch on every topic relevant to work in one book, much less just in one chapter on management. All that we really need to know is found in Ephesians 6:9. It reminds those who have authority at work to treat their workers well, without threatening them, "because you know that both their Master and yours is in heaven, and there is no favoritism with Him."

As we relate to others on the job, there will inevitably be those people who are "difficult" or people whose weaknesses are more challenging to us. God reminds us that we are to show equal regard for everyone as individuals created by God, even if they annoy us with their immaturity or personality differences.

The head coach is always making calls that highlight His kindness. May we do the same in our coaching roles, pointing our teams to the kind of success that finds favor in His sight.

CHAPTER 13

The Open Nest

When my father, a Korean War fighter pilot, retired from the Air Force in his early forties, he spent a few years transitioning to a new career in energy management. I was in second grade when he retired—old enough to know that most fathers were not at home as often as he was and young enough to be unfamiliar with the correct terminology for this stage of life.

When my teacher asked me what my father did, I proudly responded: "He doesn't have a job. He's retarded."

And followed it with a big—and uncomprehending—smile.

Later, when I was in college, there was a campaign in the women's studies department to celebrate the post-childbearing years in a woman's life. They wanted a term that would recognize the freedom and opportunities in this season, as well as the life wisdom that had been attained. They wanted a way to elevate wise elders to their natural and honored place in society. So they decided to reclaim a Middle English term—*crone*.

CRONE?! Like that was ever gonna fly!

When talking about new seasons of life, success is all about using the right term for the right situation. That's why years ago I jettisoned use of the term "empty nest." One of my friends called it "open nest" and I latched onto that phrase immediately. It's a much more optimistic description. In the open-nest season, you may be transitioning from a full-time homemaking season and looking to enter the job market again. Or you may be ready to retire from a full-time career and transition to volunteer work. Or you may be interested in a little of both. Either way, you have new opportunities opening up and, Lord willing, the time and energy to invest all you have learned into new adventures and new people to nurture.

So, in this, our final chapter, Nora and I want to share the examples of several friends who are flourishing in the *open-nest* season. For our younger readers, we hope this chapter will inspire you to think ahead to the second half of life and dream about the possibilities. (And if you use the word *crone* to describe anyone even one day older than you are, expect a prompt smackdown.)

Still Every Age

In her book *A Circle of Quiet*, author Madeleine L'Engle wrote about the advantage of perspective and memory in midlife:

> I am still every age that I have been. Because I was
> once a child, I am always a child. Because I was once
> a searching adolescent, given to moods and ecstasies,
> these are still a part of me, and always will be. . . .
> Far too many people misunderstand what *putting
> away childish things* means, and think that forgetting
> what it is like to think and feel and touch and smell
> and taste and see and hear like a three-year-old or a
> thirteen-year-old or a twenty-three-year-old means
> being a grown up. . . . Instead of which, if I can retain
> a child's awareness and joy, and *be* fifty-one, then I
> will really learn what it means to be a grownup. I still
> have a long way to go.[1]

At sixty, Linda embodies this joyful paradox. I don't think I've ever had a conversation with her where I haven't laughed until I cried. Stand-up comics would kill for her escapades. Yet Linda is also a relatively new widow, having lost her husband to ALS (Lou Gehrig's Disease) only a few years ago. After decades in the same town and in the same church, she decided to move to a smaller city where she could help start a new church.

"Here, I'm just Linda," she says. "Back home, I was Ray's widow. We were a couple who did everything together. After he died, I wondered if

I could ever be used again. What was I going to do as a single person? You feel like your arms have been cut off."

Yet when I called her to do this interview, she apologized for being exhausted: "I got home around 1:00 a.m. last night. I was doing a Bible Study at a strip club."

Of course. That's how Linda rolls. Only a few months in town, and she's already part of a serious outreach ministry to women in the adult entertainment industry.

"It's interesting how God has changed my life," she muses. "I don't have a husband or children at home. So I have the time to do this kind of ministry, and hopefully the wisdom I didn't have as a younger woman."

Linda has always had interesting stories. For twenty years, she was a sign-language interpreter for the CIA. But once she and Ray were married, she scaled down to working two to three days a week, coordinating her schedule with the demands of Ray's home renovation business. When they adopted their three children, she left the CIA and dropped down to one day a week as a freelance interpreter. She found she could work shorter hours and charge higher rates, which gave her a measure of freedom to work around her personal priorities.

"I wanted to give my best energy to home and church," she says. "My work was a means to help my family. I wasn't emotionally invested in it."

During the last five years of Ray's life, as his illness progressed, she realized she needed to get ready for life as a widow. So she got recertified in American Sign Language (ASL) and began working for a large company so she could be part of a good health insurance plan. Looking back, she wished she hadn't let her certification lapse when she was busy raising her family, because it was much harder to get recertified: "My advice to younger women is to keep current whatever certifications you have, so you can jump right back in whenever you need to."

It was hard for Linda to go back to full-time work when Ray was sick. But she persevered: "I opened every door I could. Even if it didn't work, it sometimes led to another door. I've seen young people get discouraged. Just have a 'can do' attitude; you never know what it will lead to."

When she moved to her new hometown, she did a lot of research online and called ahead to some interpreters, asking about the market for ASL interpreters. She contacted every agency and filled out reams of paperwork. Hospitals have a major need for interpreters, so she had to get TB tests and numerous vaccinations. Then, to do medical interpretation, she also needed errors and omissions professional liability insurance. It was a lot of work to set up her new business, but now she only needs to book three to four days a week to stay afloat.

One of her favorite assignments is to interpret for students at an elementary school. "I love being in the school," she says. "Doing this work, I'm not isolated to my own generation."

Linda is looking forward to the future. She is going to the gym to invest in her health and stamina. She is serving in her local church and hosting many events at her home, cultivating new friendships. She is investing in an outreach ministry. She is looking forward to the day her three adult children get married and have children of their own. But she is not slowing down just yet.

"It's a great half of life," she says. "I feel like I have more wisdom now and more life experience to bring to any situation. I am hopeful for the future."

Stretching Forward

But sometimes hope for the future is a harder struggle. In her book *The Undistracted Widow*, Carol Cornish asks some good questions to those who have reached the second half of life and experienced unexpected change: "Do we have anything to stretch toward?" She continues:

> On the gearshift of life, there is no reverse. The only
> choice is to go forward. The good thing about this
> road trip is that God is in the driver's seat. He knows
> the way to where we are going, so we cannot get lost.
> But sometimes we feel like we're sitting on the side of
> the road in a disabled vehicle. It looks like life is passing us by.[2]

For some of our friends, the Great Recession accelerated that sensation of life passing by as the poor economy upended many jobs. Even years later, the effects continue. In a recent survey of older workers (late fifties to early sixties) who were laid off during the recession, just one in six had found another job, and half of that group had accepted pay cuts. Fourteen percent of the reemployed said the pay in their new job was less than half of what they earned in their previous job.[3]

In Nancy's case, an unexpected illness compounded this economic upheaval. Nancy was in her early fifties when the Great Recession hit and her husband's health unraveled. "I never thought that after twenty-five years as a homemaker, I would have to work because my husband couldn't," she says.

Her husband is a man with an incredible work ethic; it was shocking to his family when he spiraled into a deep depression and could not find a new job. He went from being an executive to pruning trees around the neighborhood. As a result, Nancy went from being a wife and mother, to a caregiver and breadwinner.

She says, "Before my husband got sick, he and I talked about me going back to work. I was angry about it because I thought he didn't value what I did all those years at home." Despite her mixed emotions, she started training to become a yoga teacher.

During his illness she says, "I was grateful for my job. It saved me." Her job helped her to get out of the house and provided a balance to the stress of caring for her husband. Nancy's husband slowly recovered and found a job again, but Nancy continues to work, building her small business as a yoga instructor. Her life now is different than what she once anticipated it would be, but she said she is starting to see how God was stretching her to grow again even in the reversals of life.

Now, she really enjoys the way her work has opened up new relationships and opportunities. She is able to give financially to support different causes and ministries with the additional income; and, she has new friends with whom to share the gospel, like in her book club.

Like Nancy, Jane's husband was also the one to jump-start the conversation about what to do in the open-nest season. When their first child left for college, he told Jane that he wanted her to find a job when she finished homeschooling their youngest child.

"For years I struggled with this, wanting to stay at home and minister to others, or perhaps to do volunteer work in our community. I wanted God to change my husband's heart about it, but He changed mine, instead," she says.

n looking at this next stage with excitement. By the time I
homeschooling, I will be fifty-two. The last time I considered what I wanted to be or do when I grew up, I was twenty-two. Now I
know more about myself, and more about the world. I understand much
more about how I am called as a believer to interact with the world, and
so much more about my own gifts and abilities—and, more importantly,
about my limitations. When I was twenty-two, I didn't know I had any!
God has awakened passions within me that I didn't know existed thirty
years ago."

I last saw Jane at a conference for Christians in the workplace. She
came up to me with great excitement to announce she is considering a
position with a relief organization that helps women and girls around
the world. She is looking forward to investing what she has learned as a
wife and mother to make a difference for those in developing nations.

Transitioning into the workplace over fifty is a challenge, but it's
not impossible. Research suggests that this coming decade may reverse
that trend, as huge numbers of Boomers retire and employers scramble
to fill in the thinning ranks with the smaller labor pool of Generation
X. One study estimated that by 2018 there could be more than five
million unfilled jobs in the United States due to this population shift.
Therefore, employers will need to consider how to attract older workers
with different backgrounds who are looking for "encore careers"—paid
work that generally revolves around improving the quality of life in our
local communities or elsewhere. Workers will also need to get qualified
for these careers: Of the nearly 7 million jobs projected to be added to
social sector industries by 2018, 3.5 million jobs will be in health care
and social assistance.[4]

But you don't have to pursue an "encore career" to be productive in
the open-nest season—current research shows that many older workers
are becoming independent contractors in their own fields. More than
7 in 10 American employers are presently concerned about the loss of
talented older workers, and 30 percent are already hiring retirees as con-
sultants or in part-time jobs.[5] The wisdom of age is often a valuable, and
marketable, resource.

However, the open-nest season is not always about working in the
marketplace. Productivity in this time may be a reversal from years of
frenetic activity to something more contemplative and targeted.

Ramping Down

At fifty-eight, Mary's résumé is simply too long to recite. Most recently she worked at a poverty relief organization, where her husband, Robert, sixty-two, is still employed. The route they took to get there, however, was colorful and varied.

They started out as teachers in Alaska because Robert had been an art major. They returned to their home state of Colorado to work at a Bible camp for four years. That was followed by a landfill business with extended family members that failed fairly quickly. They had to borrow money to move to Phoenix where they started a banking business, developing software that they eventually sold to a corporate bank card processing company. They used that money to get into the real estate business. "But all along, we were always doing ministry," she says.

To wit, at various points in her life, Mary has been a women's ministry director for a local church. She worked with Prison Fellowship. She worked with a mentoring program for homeless families. She got involved with orphans of AIDS in Africa—and then was a part of a team that started the U.S. arm of a ministry based in South Africa. Then she began raising funds for poverty relief by participating in several international treks before landing in the church engagement division of a nonprofit ministry—her most recent position.

"Yeah, I'm a little tired," she says, laughing. "But we were pretty naïve about life in our twenties, so we had to wait for about thirty years to do what we're doing now."

In the midst of her swirl of activity, Mary had an epiphany: it was time to ramp down.

"I would be on deadline for a work project and my grandchildren would Skype me and I would be trying to act relaxed and not pressured by their interruption," she recalls. "Then the caregiver would call with a problem about my mother. Then one of our rental properties would become vacant and need my attention. All of this plus trying to do my job was too much. What I really want to do at this stage of my life is be a mentor to younger people, not create my own work. That's when I realized I had this 'other productivity' in my life that needed to be tended. There were things coming due, things I could harvest."

Mary felt she had too many things fired up at the same level. With both of them busy at work, she realized she was sapping strength from Robert and that she needed to support him a little bit more. So she decided to step down.

"I think some of us Boomers aren't doing that—we're not moving over and making room for others," she says. "Boomers don't know how to be productive unless they are working. I have friends who are set for life financially but are still working crazy schedules. We Boomers just keep it ratcheted really high."

After stepping down, Mary invested some time to reflect upon and analyze her gifts, strengths, and life experience. She identified two key goals for this stage of life with her husband—their income streams need to be simplified and their relationships need more investment.

"I see life as having an exploratory stage, a productive stage, an effective stage, and a mentoring stage," she says. "I'm in the mentoring stage now. So I asked myself, what is this stage in life all about? It's not going to look like my forties even though I still have a lot of energy."

Mary and Robert have several good friends who are considering a different way of living in the future. She doesn't want to be isolated and in her eighties, living alone, like she sees among her own relatives and friends. Living communally seems more thoughtful and resourceful to Mary. It will likely require a move. They have a large farmhouse in Colorado that they have been restoring over the last few years. It has seventeen acres and requires much maintenance. "To get out of our driveway when it snows, we have to get on the tractor—and that's not appropriate for this stage of life," she says laughing.

She has enjoyed using this home for hospitality but doesn't think it will be useful for their streamlined future. Instead, they have considered finding a home that addresses many of the questions and concerns they have about the future—maybe a home with multiple master suites that could accommodate other couples interested in communal living, a dwelling that provides cost savings and caregiving opportunities, and minimizes isolation. It's just an idea at this point, but one she is giving careful consideration to developing.

"I think in the church we teach a lot about our roles as young wives and mothers, but we don't talk about this stage. Maybe we talk about the joy of grandmothers, but not all the rest of it. The fact is, it can be a really hard stage—there can be a lot of disappointments for people. So I would say to my friends, just take a step back and take a deep breath, and look at all the things you have going on in your life and that you aren't managing well. Some of these women, their husbands need more support than they think they do."

She adds: "Then think about what your legacy is going to be. I've always been an advocate for women—it didn't matter if it was because of AIDS in Africa, or poverty in Bangladesh, or homeless women or women in prison, or just a bunch of women hiking in Colorado—it's always just been a part of my life. I expect that will continue but in a more focused way."

An Advocate for Women

Being an advocate for women and girls in the open-nest season is not a new concept. When Christianity arrived on the scene, it was unparalleled in valuing women who were in this stage of life, typically widows. "Nothing in Judaism or paganism paralleled Christianity's exaltation of widowhood," historian Diana Severance writes. "However, widows were not simply cared for by the Church; they were also important to the functioning of the church. They were given the responsibility of nursing the sick, caring for the poor, dispensing the alms of the Church, and evangelizing pagan women."[6]

This great ministry need continues today, both in our own towns and around the world. It is a strategically important time for women to be involved in outreach and ministry to other women. We who have the message that God made women in His image need to be on the frontlines in places where simply being born female puts a life at risk. There are women and girls suffering economic and legal injustice in their nations, denied education, opportunities to work, maternal healthcare, and even their lives. Women are aborting their female fetuses in vast numbers because they have believed the *demonic lie* of their cultures that women are not equal in worth to men. This calls for bold women armed with the truth of Scripture to get involved and fight for those who suffer such injustices.

This is a topic worthy of an entire book itself—and much has already been written on it—but we offer it with fervent exhortation to any woman who feels lost or useless in the open-nest years. You have a life *full* of wisdom and experience to invest! You have *decades* of testimonies about the faithfulness of God! And there is a dying world that needs to know what you know. They need your help, your mentoring, and your message.

Many of us can be tempted to feel that our lives only serve as a warning to others. I saw that statement on a sarcastic poster once and laughed out loud. Yep, I can already identify. But what is true of me is not true of *God*. He wastes nothing, creating beauty out of the ashes of our failures and weaknesses. As Peter said in Acts 3:6 (NIV), "Silver or gold I do not have, but what I have I give you. In the name of Jesus Christ of Nazareth, walk." We possess things of far greater value than silver and gold: we have faith. The longer we walk with the Lord, in effect the more we have of Him to give to others—more answered prayers, more stories of His provision, more quiet confidence that He is true to His Word.

The Sacrifices of Love

Dealing with reversals in your life, finding new jobs, or pursuing a new passion takes courage in this stage of life. It can also be really hard to slow down, if that's what God is calling you to do. No matter what age you are, it's important to take stock of where you have been and where you are going. More importantly, this creates an opportunity to consider how the Lord has been working in your life by looking at His past faithfulness. Isaiah 46:9–10 says: "Remember what happened long ago, for I am God, and there is no other; I am God, and no one is like Me. I declare the end from the beginning, and from long ago what is not yet done, saying: My plan will take place, and I will do all My will."

Many of the challenges of developing an "open-nest" mentality involve evaluating goals and roles. Our goal in this book was to dispel a "one-size-fits-all" model idea about women's lives and their productivity. This includes dispelling some ideas that this time of your life should be about leisure or ease.

Now, we are not saying that you should continue to work as hard as you did when you were young. But we are saying that you should continue to do work that has real meaning and value. When we consider the legacies we are leaving, we need to evaluate our work, not just from a career perspective, but from how we have invested into our eternal roles, those works of lasting significance.

While the temptation may be to coast, these are years to continue to press into God and His Word, prayer, and fellowship. In a prophetic passage in Isaiah 32 about a messianic King who rules His transformed people, there is a warning specifically to women about complacency. It says, "Rise up, you women who are at ease, hear my voice; you complacent daughters, give ear to my speech" (v. 9 ESV). Amid a general call to repentance, spiritually heedless women are given a particular warning about complacency.

The biblical model challenges us to continue being ambitious, but in a way that brings glory to God's eternal purposes. Our time and energy are resources to be invested, not limitations to hoard for personal benefit. They are to be cultivated and given to others. This might mean that you spend time mentoring others, as Titus 2 commands older women to do. Or it might mean investing into your marriage in a new way. For many, it could involve giving time to your church and community. Always, it means sharing the gospel with others, including friends, neighbors, and grandchildren.

There is no promise of rest, yet. But the final words of that passage in Isaiah 32 offer us a glimmer of God's rewards for combating complacency by investing in the eternal while we still have the time and energy.

> "And the effect of righteousness will be peace, and the
> result of righteousness, quietness and trust forever.
> My people will abide in a peaceful habitation, in
> secure dwellings and in quiet resting places." (Isa.
> 32:17–18 ESV)

While God does not promise a gorgeous retirement home for all, He does promise peace, security, and rest for those who trust in Him.

Your time in the paid labor force may be drawing to an end, but your productivity could continue until your last breath. Your fruitfulness is not a result of your effort, but it is a gift of grace. As John Piper writes, "Knowing that we have an infinitely satisfying and everlasting inheritance in God just over the horizon of life makes us jealous in our few remaining years here to spend ourselves in the sacrifices of love, not the accumulation of comforts."[7]

As we do so, there is the glorious promise from Scripture of evergreen fruitfulness.

> The righteous thrive like a palm tree and grow like
> a cedar tree in Lebanon. Planted in the house of the
> LORD, they thrive in the courts of our God. They
> will still bear fruit in old age, healthy and green, to
> declare: "The LORD is just; He is my rock, and there is
> no unrighteousness in Him." (Ps. 92:12–15)

Our prayer today and for every day yet to come is this: *Lord, here is a new day given to me by You. Your mercies are new this morning. There are new things to be done, and new lessons to be learned. Help me to use this day properly as I head for home.*[8]

Acknowledgments

Writing is a lonely experience that requires weeks and months of enforced solitude to be productive. To all of our friends and family who supported us through prayer and cheerful check-ins while we were missing in action, please receive our deep appreciation. But there are a few individuals who should be thanked by name, so here are those shout-outs . . .

We are both grateful for the gracious support and patience of our editor, Jennifer Lyell. She is a true collaborator and friend!

We are also indebted to our pastor, Eric Simmons, for suggesting that this book be written, and then preaching many Sunday messages that shaped our ideas—especially the concept of rest.

Special thanks goes to the First Draft Team of volunteers who graciously found things to encourage as well as correct while reading rambling early editions of this book: Todd Twining, Nancy Lotinsky, Jim McCulley, Emily Davis, Kari Faherty, Colin Black, Mindy Hemmelman, Tony and Karalee Reinke, Nikki Lewis, Jane Wandell, Jill Nyhus, Candice Watters, Cara Habbegger, Becky Ross, Rachel Ellis, Christina Smart, Janelle Shank, Emily Jansen, and David Lam.

I (Nora) first would like to thank my husband. My involvement in this book is all his doing, as I like to remind him, because he prayed that my ambition would match his own and encouraged me to pursue this project. I only hope that we can continue to grow in love (and ambition) together as much as we have these first eight years together; I can't wait for the adventure to continue. Carolyn and I benefited from your strategic brilliance, your candor, and keeping us together through this project.

For this book, I must acknowledge that the women whose names and lineage I share. Thank you to my grandmothers and mothers and sisters; they are among the most brave and godly women I know. Thank you to my mom, Susan, and my mother-in-law, Janis, for all of your inspiration and support as well as your legacy of faith.

The other people who we owe thanks to for this book are all the women whose friendships and stories we have shared. Particularly, I owe a debt of gratitude to my friend, Becky, who kept me sane and laughing through some of my more difficult years and struggles. Other friends, old and new, were invaluable resources for this book, and we could not have done it without your faithful readership.

Lastly, I want to thank my friend and coauthor, Carolyn, for her encouragement when I was single, sad, and confused about life. You inspired me then and you continue to teach me today. Thank you for being a mother to so many of us along our journey.

I (Carolyn) could never have finished this project without Nora's cheerful encouragement and diligent labors. From start to finish, your faith toward God refreshed me. When we *both* were on deadline, you were the one to make me meals, bring me flowers, and remind me that God's grace is sufficient for the daunting task before us. You have been a generous (and *awesome*!) partner in this venture.

But my thanks also go to my colleagues at Citygate Films: Suzanne Glover, Brad Allgood, and Daniel Pinto. Writing a book about work while working long hours on film projects is just plain *crazy*. Thank you for picking up all the loose ends and doing it so cheerfully. You make work fun.

I am most grateful for the support of my family, especially my father who read through every chapter of this book with his outstanding copyediting skills. (However, any remaining errors are all mine.) My sisters, Alice and Beth, should know that their fruitful examples of being hardworking mothers have shaped my thoughts on this subject for many years. I love you all!

Finally, I give thanks to my mother for the love she invested in our family. I miss you terribly, Mom, but I look forward to seeing you one day in heaven as together we praise the Lamb!

No list of acknowledgments is complete without praise for our Lord and Savior, Jesus Christ, whose sustaining grace kept His weak creatures alive and functioning on deadline. We offer our labors here with thanks for the love we have received from Him who is "gracious and merciful, slow to anger and abounding in steadfast love."

Notes

Preface

1. Carolyn McCulley, *Did I Kiss Marriage Goodbye? Trusting God with a Hope Deferred* (Wheaton, IL: Crossway Books, 2004).

2. Carolyn McCulley, *Radical Womanhood: Feminine Faith in a Feminist World* (Chicago, IL: Moody Publishers, 2008).

Chapter 1

1. Christine Garwood, *Flat Earth: The History of an Infamous Idea* (New York: Thomas Dunne Books, St. Martin's Press, 2007), 20.

2. Stephen Jay Gould, "The Late Birth of a Flat Earth," *Dinosaur in a Haystack: Reflections in Natural History* (New York: Crown, 1996), 38–52.

Chapter 2

1. Stephanie Coontz, *Marriage, a History: How Love Conquered Marriage* (New York: Penguin Books, 2005), 251–52.

2. Ibid., 231.

3. Ibid., 232.

4. Ibid., 233.

5. Ruth Schwartz Cowan, "Less Work for Mother?" *American Heritage Magazine,* September/October 1987, Volume 38, Issue 6, http://www.american heritage.com/content/less-work-mother?page=3.

6. The Pop History Dig website, "Rosie the Riveter" article, http://www .pophistorydig.com/?p=877, accessed 5/28/12.

7. Abdul Alkalimat and Associates, *Intro to Afro-American Studies: A Peoples College Primer* (Chicago: Twenty-first Century Books and Publications, 1984), chapter 11, http://eblackstudies.org/intro/chapter11.htm.

8. Betsy Israel, *Bachelor Girl: The Secret History of Single Women in the Twentieth Century* (New York: William Morrow/HarperCollins, 2002), 165.

9. Ibid., 167.

10. Coontz, *Marriage, a History*, 235.

11. Glenna Matthews, *"Just a Housewife": The Rise and Fall of Domesticity in America* (New York: Oxford University Press, 1987), 217.

12. Ibid., 218–19.

13. Stephanie Coontz, *A Strange Stirring: The Feminine Mystique and American Women at the Dawn of the 1960s* (New York: Basic Books, 2012), excerpted from "The Unliberated '60s" chapter (Kindle edition).

14. Coontz, *Marriage, a History*, 254.

15. The American Experience (PBS) program "The Pill." Historical timeline published by PBS on http://www.pbs.org/wgbh/amex/pill/timeline/timeline2.html and accessed June 2, 2012.

16. Coontz, *Marriage, a History*, 258–59.

17. Jessica Yellin, "Single, Female and Desperate No More," *The New York Times*, June 4, 2006.

18. Coontz, *Marriage, a History*, 284–85.

19. Ibid., 291.

20. Hanna Rosin, "The End of Men," *The Atlantic*, July/August 2010.

Chapter 3

1. Rudolf K. Markwald and Marilynn Morris Markwald, *Katharina von Bora: A Reformation Life* (St. Louis: Concordia Publishing House, 2002), 63.

2. Ibid., 70.

3. Ibid., 81–82.

4. Ibid., 129.

5. Ibid., 130.

6. Marilyn Yalom, *A History of the Wife* (New York: Harper Collins Publishers, 2001), 98, 105.

7. Gene Edward Veith, "Our Calling and God's Glory," *Modern Reformation*, Nov./Dec. 2007, http://www.modernreformation.org/default.php?page=articledisplay&var1=ArtRead&var2=881.

8. Ibid.

9. Ibid.

10. Elizabeth D. Dodds, *Marriage to a Difficult Man* (Laurel, MS: Audubon Press, 2004), 36.

11. Ibid., 91.

12. Diana Lynn Severance, *Feminine Threads: Women in the Tapestry of Christian History* (Glasgow: Christian Focus, 2011), 224.

13. Nancy Pearcey, *Total Truth* (Wheaton, IL: Crossway Books, 2004), 328–29.

14. Ibid., 327.

15. Carol Berkin, *Revolutionary Mothers* (New York: Vintage Books, 2005), 17.

16. Jack Lynch, "Every Man Able to Read," *Colonial Williamsburg Journal,* Winter 2011. Archived at http://www.history.org/foundation/journal/winter11/literacy.cfm.

17. Harriet Hanson Robinson, *Loom and Spindle or Life Among the Early Mill Girls* (New York: T. Y. Crowell, 1898), 83–86, as posted on http://historymatters.gmu.edu/d/5714/.

18. Thomas Dublin, "Women, Work and Protest in the Early Lowell Mills," *Labor History* (United Kingdom: Carfax Publishing, 1975), 99–116. See http://invention.smithsonian.org/centerpieces/whole_cloth/u2ei/u2materials/dublin.html.

19. Nancy F. Cott, "Young Women in the Second Great Awakening in New England," *Feminist Studies* Vol. 3, No. 1/2 (Autumn 1975), 15.

20. Charles A. Maxfield, "The Formation and Early History of the American Board of Commissioners for Foreign Missions," as presented to Union Theological Seminary for dissertation in 1995. See http://www.maxfieldbooks.com/ABCFM.html.

21. Matthews, *"Just a Housewife,"* 49, 51.

22. Severance, *Feminine Threads*, 270–71.

23. John Angell James, *Female Piety: A Young Woman's Friend and Guide* (Morgan, PA: Soli Deo Gloria Publications, 1999), 175.

24. Nancy Pearcey, "Is Love Enough? Recreating the Economic Base of the Family," *The Family in America*, January 1990 Vol. 4, No. I, http://www.leaderu.com/orgs/arn/pearcey/np_familyinamerica.htm.

25. Betsy Israel, *Bachelor Girl: The Secret History of Single Women in the Twentieth Century* (New York: William Morrow, 2002), 57.

26. Ibid., 30.

27. Jim Downs, "Dying for Freedom," *The New York Times* Opinionator, Jan. 5, 2013, http://opinionator.blogs.nytimes.com/2013/01/05/dying-for-freedom.

28. Coontz, *Marriage, a History*, 192.

29. Israel, *Bachelor Girl*, 97.

30. Severance, *Feminine Threads*, 287.

31. Yalom, *A History of the Wife*, 288–89.

32. Coontz, *Marriage, a History*, 209.

33. Israel, *Bachelor Girl*, 151.

34. Coontz, *Marriage, a History*, 320.

Chapter 4

1. Bruce W. Winter, *Roman Wives, Roman Widows: The Appearance of New Women and the Pauline Communities* (Grand Rapids, MI: William B. Eerdmans Publishing Co., 2003), xii.

2. John MacArthur, *Twelve Extraordinary Women* (Nashville: Thomas Nelson, 2005), 190.

3. Ibid., 191.

4. Howard F. Vos, *Nelson's New Illustrated Bible Manners & Customs* (Nashville: Thomas Nelson Publishers, 1999), 630.

5. MacArthur, *Twelve Extraordinary Women*, 196.

6. Winter, *Roman Wives, Roman Widows*, 42.

7. Ibid., 51.

8. Ibid., 53.

9. Diana Lynn Severance, *Feminine Threads: Women in the Tapestry of Christian History* (Glasgow: Christian Focus, 2011), 31.

10. Barry Danylak, *Redeeming Singleness: How the Storyline of Scripture Affirms the Single Life* (Wheaton, IL: Crossway Books, 2010), 80–81.

11. Elizabeth Wayland Barber, *Women's Work: The First 20,000 Years* (New York: W. W. Norton & Co., 1994), 29–31.

12. The *ESV Study Bible*, English Standard Version (Wheaton, IL: Crossway Bibles, 2008).

Chapter 5

1. Leland Ryken, *Redeeming the Time* (Grand Rapids: Baker Books, 1995), 177.

2. Leland Ryken, *Work and Leisure in Christian Perspective* (Multnomah Press: Portland, OR, 1987), 129.

3. The *ESV Study Bible*, English Standard Version (Wheaton, IL: Crossway Bibles, 2008), 52.

4. Jon Huntsinger, *The Trees Will Clap Their Hands: A Garden Theology* (Bloomington, IN: Westbow Press, 2012), 9.

5. Martin Luther, "The Babylonian Captivity of the Church," *Three Treatises* (Philadelphia: Fortress Press, 1990), 202–3.

6. Ryken, *Redeeming the Time*, 76.

7. Gustaf Wingren, *Luther on Vocation*, trans. Carl C. Rasmussen (Eugene, OR: Wipf & Stock Publishers, 1957), 8.

8. Ibid., 72.

9. Ryken, *Redeeming the Time*, 165.

Chapter 6

1. "Bring Back the 40-Hour Workweek," Sara Robinson, *Salon* magazine, posted Wednesday, March 14, 2012 on http://www.salon.com/2012/03/14/bring_back_the_40_hour_work_week.

2. Tim Challies, "Workaholism," from the Challies.com blog, published March 27, 2012, http://www.challies.com/writings/podcast/workaholism transcribed from a podcast on 03/27/12.

3. Tim Keller, "Wisdom and Sabbath Rest," published on Q Ideas for the Common Good, http://www.qideas.org/blog/wisdom-and-sabbath-rest.aspx.

4. Ibid.

Chapter 7

1. Jill U. Adams, "Health Effects of Retirement Have Proved Hard for Researchers to Assess," *The Washington Post*, February 25, 2013, http://www.washingtonpost.com/national/health-science/health-effects-of-retirement-have-proved-hard-for-researchers-to-assess/2013/02/25/4999e4f6-698f-11e2-ada3-d86a4806d5ee_story.html.

Chapter 8

1. Sheryl Sandberg, "Sheryl Sandberg Sees Global 'Ambition Gap' for Women," a talk recorded Jan. 27, 2012 at the World Economic Forum. Posted by Bloomberg TV at http://www.bloomberg.com/video/85189956/.

2. *Holman Christian Standard Study Bible.* Word Study on Genesis 1:28. Strong's Hebrew Greek Dictionary, Hebrew 433, http://www.mystudybible.com, accessed 5/9/2012.

3. "Millennials and the Corporate World: Executive Summary," Bentley University of Waltham, MA, http://www.bentley.edu/centers/center-for-women-and-business/millennials-and-corporate-world.

4. Alister Chapman, *Godly Ambition: John Stott and the Evangelical Movement* (New York: Oxford University Press, 2012), 155.

5. Betty Friedan in a 1981 *New York Times* interview (October 19, 1981 *New York Times* books by Nan Robertson "Betty Friedan Ushers In a 'Second Stage'" as archived on http://www.nytimes.com/books/99/05/09/specials/friedan-stage.html.

6. *The Bible Background Commentary*, 375.

7. Although the origin of this quote is unclear, its attribution to Elliot and consistency of phrasing speaks to its veracity.

Chapter 9

1. North Carolina State University (October 10, 2012). "Parenting more important than schools to academic achievement, study finds." *ScienceDaily*. Retrieved March 9, 2013, from http://www.sciencedaily.com /releases/2012/10/121010112540.htm.

2. U.S. Census Bureau, Current Population Survey, 2010 Annual Social and Economic Supplement, http://www.census.gov/hhes/www/cpstables /032010/perinc/new03_019.htm.

3. Quoting former UN Special Rapporteur on the Right to Education, Katarina Tomasevski. From her report on education, http://www.katarina tomasevski.com.

4. "Goal 2: Achieve Universal Primary Education," Fact Sheet of the United Nations Summit, September 20–22, 2010, http://www.un.org /millenniumgoals/pdf/MDG_FS_2_EN.pdf.

5. Robbye Fox, "Teaching Kids About Money," Washington Parent blog, August 2012 entry, http://washingtonparent.com/articles/1208/kids-and -money.php.

Chapter 10

1. According to the *Merriam-Webster* online dictionary, http://www .merriam-webster.com/dictionary/gussy%20up.

2. Gussie Moran obituary: "Tennis star's outfits stunned spectators," *The Washington Post*, January 23, 2013, B5.

3. Shaunti Feldhahn, *For Women Only in the Workplace: What You Need to Know About How Men Think at Work* (Colorado Springs: Multnomah Books, 2011), 193.

4. Ibid., 196.

5. Ned Martel, "The Economy of Christine Lagarde," *The Washington Post,* Sept. 24, 2012, http://www.washingtonpost.com/politics/the-economy-of -christine-lagarde/2012/09/24/8d5c2b84-cd01-11e1-b7dd-ef7ef87186df_story.html.

6. Feldhahn, *For Women Only in the Workplace,* 199.

7. Lori Hollander, "The Five Truths Every Married Person Should Know about Affairs," blog post published July 21, 2011, http://www.goodtherapy.org /blog/truths-workplace-affair.

8. Gary Stoller, "Infidelity Is in the Air for Road Warriors," *USA Today*, April 23, 2007.

9. Diane Paddison, "How to Socialize with Coworkers," 4Word blog, http://www.4wordwomen.org/blog/2012/12/how-to-socialize-with-coworkers.

Chapter 11

1.Haya El Nasser "Adult kids living at home on the rise across the board," *USA Today*: 8/1/2012, http://usatoday30.usatoday.com/news/nation/story /2012-08-01/boomerang-adults-recession-kids-at-home/56623746/1, accessed 1/17/13.

2. Meghan Casserly, "Is 'Opting Out' the New American Dream for Working Women?" ForbesWomen blog, published September 12, 2012, http:// www.forbes.com/sites/meghancasserly/2012/09/12/is-opting-out-the-new -american-dream-for-working-women, accessed 1/14/13.

3. Bureau of Labor Statistics, Economic News Release: "Employment Characteristics of Families Summary," issued April 26, 2012, http://www.bls .gov/news.release/famee.nr0.htm.

4. United States Census Bureau: "Facts for Features: Mother's Day: May 8, 2011," http://www.census.gov/newsroom/releases/archives/facts_for_features _special_editions/cb11-ff07.html, accessed 1/14/13.

5. Tim Challies, "The Intrinsic Value of What You Do (Yes, You!)" 01/11/12, http://www.challies.com/articles/the-intrinsic-value-of-what-you-do -yes-you#more, accessed 02/25/2012.

6. Jim Taylor, "Myth of Multitasking," *Psychology Today* blog, March 30, 2011, http://www.psychologytoday.com/blog/the-power-prime/201103 /technology-myth-multitasking.

7. Andi Ashworth, *Real Love for Real Life* (Nashville: Rabbit Room Press, 2012), 37–38.

8. Larissa Faw, "Why Millennial Women Are Burning Out at Work at 30" ForbesWoman.com, 11/11/2011, http://www.forbes.com/sites/laris-safaw/2011/11/11/why-millennial-women-are-burning-out-at-work-by-30, accessed 2/14/12.

9. Ashworth, Real Love for Real Life, 138–39.

10. Alexandra Sifferlin, "Report: U.S. Is the 25th Best Country to Be a Mom," TIME Healthland, May 10, 2012, http://healthland.time.com/2012/05/10 /report-u-s-is-the-25th-best-country-to-be-a-mom/#ixzz2JbvAnTMw.

11. "Keeping America's Women Moving Forward," a report issued in April 2012 from the White House Council on Women and Girls, http://m.white house.gov/sites/default/files/email-files/womens_report_final_for_print.pdf.

12. "On Ramps and Off Ramps Revisited," The Center for Work-Life Policy, May 18, 2010, http://www.worklifepolicy.org/documents/Off -Ramps%20Revisited%20Release%20-%20CWLP%205.18.10.pdf.

13. Lia Macko and Kerry Rubin, *Midlife Crisis at 30* (Emmaus, PA: Rodale, 2012), 169.

14. Kate Harris, "Epiphany, Mission and Motherhood," originally published in *Comment* magazine, Jan. 29, 2010. Reposted Jan. 2012 on

the Washington Institute website, http://www.washingtoninst.org/1447/epiphany-mission-motherhood.

Chapter 12

1. Anne Somerset, *Elizabeth I* (London: Anchor Books, 2003), 727.

2. Wayne Grudem, *Evangelical Feminism and Biblical Truth* (Sisters, OR: Multnomah, 2004), 393.

3. Jack Zenger and Joseph Folkman, "Are Women Better Leaders than Men?" published on the HBR Blog Network on March 15, 2012, http://blogs.hbr.org/cs/2012/03/a_study_in_leadership_women_do.html.

4. Shaunti Feldhahn, *For Women Only in the Workplace*, 29.

5. Ibid., 61.

6. John Beeson, "Deconstructing Executive Presence," HBR Blog Network, published August 22, 2012, http://blogs.hbr.org/cs/2012/08/de-constructing_executive_pres.html.

Chapter 13

1. Madeleine L'Engle, *A Circle of Quiet* (New York: HarperOne, 1984), 199–200.

2. Carol Cornish, *The Undistracted Widow* (Wheaton, IL: Crossway Books 2010), 135, 137.

3. Catherine Rampell, "In Hard Economy for All Ages, Older Isn't Better . . . It's Brutal," *The New York Times*, Feb. 2, 2013, http://www.nytimes.com/2013/02/03/business/americans-closest-to-retirement-were-hardest-hit-by-recession.html?ref=catherinerampell&pagewanted=all.

4. Barry Bluestone and Mark Melnik, "Help Needed: The Coming Labor Shortage and How People in Encore Careers Can Help Solve it," published by the Kitty and Michael Dukakis Center for Urban and Regional Policy at Northeastern University, Boston and Civic Ventures, 2010, http://www.encore.org/files/research/JobsBluestonePaper3-5-10.pdf.

5. Michelle Singletary, "When Work Still Beckons," The Color of Money column, *The Washington Post*, Jan. 9, 2013, A11.

6. Diana Severance, *Feminine Threads*, 54.

7. John Piper, *Rethinking Retirement* (Wheaton, IL: Crossway Books, 2008), 6.

8. Carol Cornish quoting Geoff Thomas in *The Undistracted Widow*, 139.